Isaiah Reid

**Highway Hymnal**

A Choice Collection of Popular Hymns and Music

Isaiah Reid

**Highway Hymnal**
*A Choice Collection of Popular Hymns and Music*

ISBN/EAN: 9783337428174

Printed in Europe, USA, Canada, Australia, Japan

Cover: Foto ©Thomas Meinert / pixelio.de

More available books at **www.hansebooks.com**

# THE
# HIGHWAY HYMNAL,

— A —

## CHOICE COLLECTION

— OF —

# POPULAR HYMNS AND MUSIC,

### NEW AND OLD.

*Arranged for Work in Camp, Convention, Church and Home.*

 BY

## REV. ISAIAH REID AND REV. GEO. L. BROWN.

---

PUBLISHED AT THE HIGHWAY OFFICE, NEVADA, IOWA.

☞ *All rights reserved by Isaiah Reid and Geo. L. Brown.*

## PREFACE TO HIGHWAY HYMNS.

"*Whoso offereth praise glorifieth me.*" Ps. 50:23.

THE aim of this little collection is only a convenient pocket copy of the songs we usually sing at the present time in our camp and social meetings. Some words are old, some new. The people love to sing them and we love to help them by putting the words before them. We think the value of the cleansing blood is fully written therein. They are full of salvation with no "prone to wander" lines at all. Sing on, and believe on, till you enter in. And may He teach you to sing with the Spirit and with the understanding also. Your brethren in Jesus.

ISAIAH REID, H. F. ASHCRAFT, F. H. ASHCRAFT.

## PREFACE TO HIGHWAY HYMNAL.

WE claim this to be a good collection, if not the best, of *tried* hymns, and choruses. The new pieces are offered like all other new things, on trial. Attention is called to the pages containing a system of "call" and "altar" songs and choruses. Either page is worth ten times the price of the book. In your social meetings try Pisgah, Windham, Atonement, Duane Street, etc, tunes now discarded from the great church hymn books, and notice the power and majesty in them. Many do not like *spiritual* songs, on account, as they say, of their "mannerisms and flipancy." We often, as Wm. Taylor says, hear them appropriately singing;

"In vain we tune our formal songs,
In vain we strive to rise,
Hosannahs languish on our tongues,
And our devotion dies."

Let them get an experience which voices itself like this:

"My Sun no more goes down by day
My moon no more is waning
My feet ran swift the SHINING WAY
The heavenly portals gaining,"

and the sweet soul-music and stirring "Amen," of the "pilgrims" will no longer grate harshly on their ears.

*ISAIAH REID,*
*GEO. L. BROWN.*

NOTE. We have not intentionally used any copy-righted piece without permission. If any one finds his production thus used, he will please send bill for his usual price.

☞ ALL RIGHTS RESERVED.

# Highway Hmynal.

### No. 1.
## THE WHITE FLAG.

Words by D. J. MANDELL.   Music by GEO. L. BROWN.

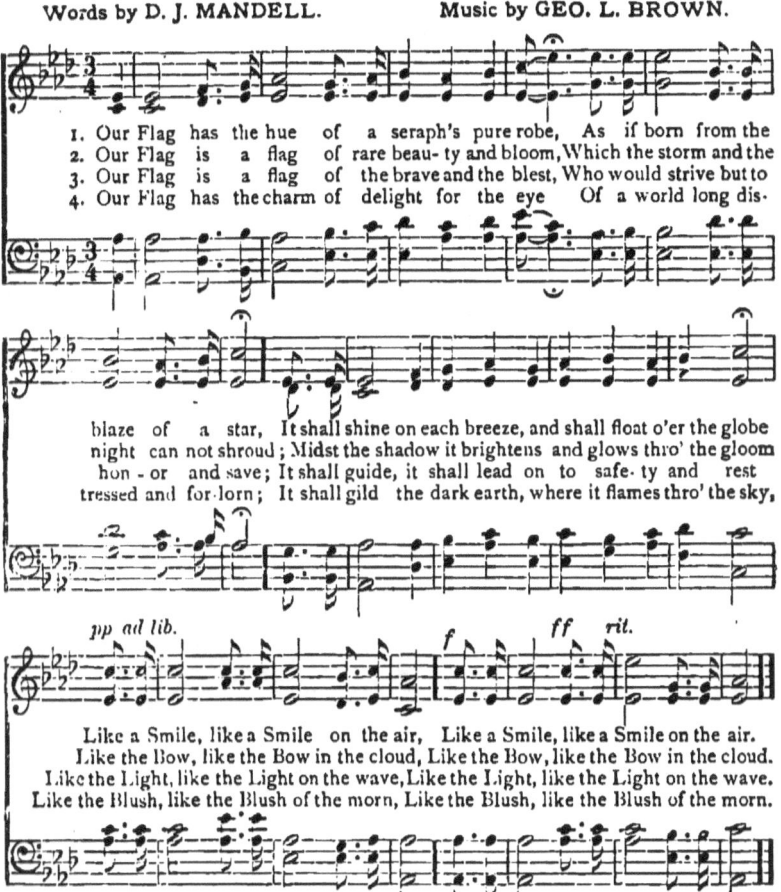

1. Our Flag has the hue of a seraph's pure robe, As if born from the blaze of a star, It shall shine on each breeze, and shall float o'er the globe Like a Smile, like a Smile on the air, Like a Smile, like a Smile on the air.
2. Our Flag is a flag of rare beauty and bloom, Which the storm and the night can not shroud; Midst the shadow it brightens and glows thro' the gloom Like the Bow, like the Bow in the cloud, Like the Bow, like the Bow in the cloud.
3. Our Flag is a flag of the brave and the blest, Who would strive but to honor and save; It shall guide, it shall lead on to safety and rest Like the Light, like the Light on the wave, Like the Light, like the Light on the wave.
4. Our Flag has the charm of delight for the eye Of a world long distressed and forlorn; It shall gild the dark earth, where it flames thro' the sky, Like the Blush, like the Blush of the morn, Like the Blush, like the Blush of the morn.

## No. 2.
## A VOICE FROM EDEN.

Music by GEO. L. BROWN.

2 I hear hope singing, sweetly singing,
  Softly in an undertone,
And singing as if God had taught it,
  "It is better farther on."

3 By night and day it sings the same song,
  Sings it while I sit alone,
And sings it so the heart may hear it:
  "It is better farther on."

4 It sits upon the grave and sings it,
  Sings it when the heart would groan,
And sings it when the shadows darken;
  "It is better farther on."

5 Still farther on! oh, how much farther?
  Count the mile-stones one by one;
No! no! no counting—only trusting:
  "It is better farther on."

## No. 3. Let me Tell the Story.

By GEO. L. BROWN.

1 In the val-ley of sad-ness and sor-row I remained ma-ny wea-risome years, Vain-ly try-ing en-chantment to bor-row; Ev-er reap-ing un-kind-ness and tears. Now I stand on the Rock, shouting glory! . . All my soul filled with gladness su-preme; . . And to-day let me tell the sweet old sto-ry, I am washed in the soul-cleansing stream.

2 When for par-don I of-fered his mer-it, Christ removed ev'-ry dark, guilt-y stain; When I knelt for the gift of the Spir-it, Then bestowed he God's im-age a-gain.

3
So I walk every day by the River,
 Whose sweet waters are life to my soul,
And the gift I enjoy in the Giver,
 Since in Jesus I'm happy and whole.

4
Little ones, let us journey together,
 Let us shine in the Lord's perfect love;
Let us labor and pray for each other
 Till the angels shall waft us above.

3 Why linger a nursling, so feeble,
  When the Master is needing a man?
Our King's is a bountiful table,
  Let mortal despoil it who can.

4 Ye poor, wretched starvelings of Zion,
  The Father commands you to eat,
Here is meat that came forth from our Lion,
Here are garners of barley and wheat

5 Why build ye of straw and of stubble,
  With silver in reach of your hand?
In the great day of burning and trouble,
  Your building of straw will not stand.

6 Who eats the sweet manna may labor,
  Who labors way wear a bright crown;
Go eat, and then strengthen thy neighbor,
  E'er thy day and probation are flown.

## Come Thou Fount.

1
Come Thou fount of every blessing,
 Tune my heart to sing Thy grace;
Streams of mercy never ceasing,
 Call for songs of loudest praise;

2
Teach me some melodious sonnet,
 Sung by flaming tongues above;
Praise the mount, I'm fixed upon it!
 Mount of Thy redeeming love.

3
Here I'll raise my Ebenezer,
 Hither by Thy help I'm come;
And I hope by Thy good pleasure,
 Safely to arrive at home.

4
Jesus sought me when a stranger,
 Wandering from the fold of God;
He to rescue me from danger,
 Interposed His precious blood.

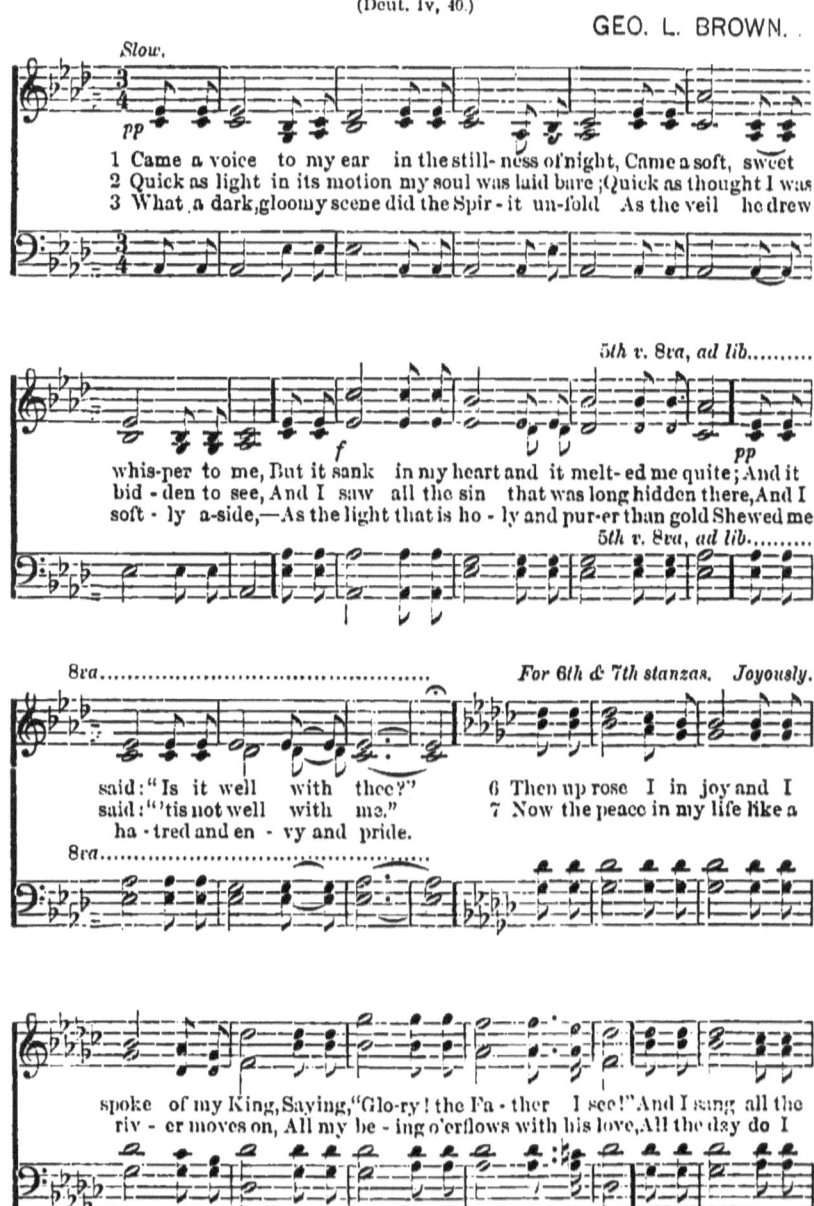

## Highway Hymnal.

day as the sanc-ti-fied sing, And I said, "IT IS WELL WITH ME."
pray and I won-der how soon Shall I sing with the an-gels a - bove?

4 Came again the still voice as I bowed in deep woe,
And it said: "I have somewhat for thee—
Will you leave all you love?—will you go where I go?
*Will you dare to be nothing for Me?"*

5 Then I trembled with fear, but I spoke all my soul,
And I answered: "Lord help me—*I will.*"
Came the voice once again, and it said "BE YE WHOLE,"
And I drank of His fulness my fill.

### No. 7. Purity.

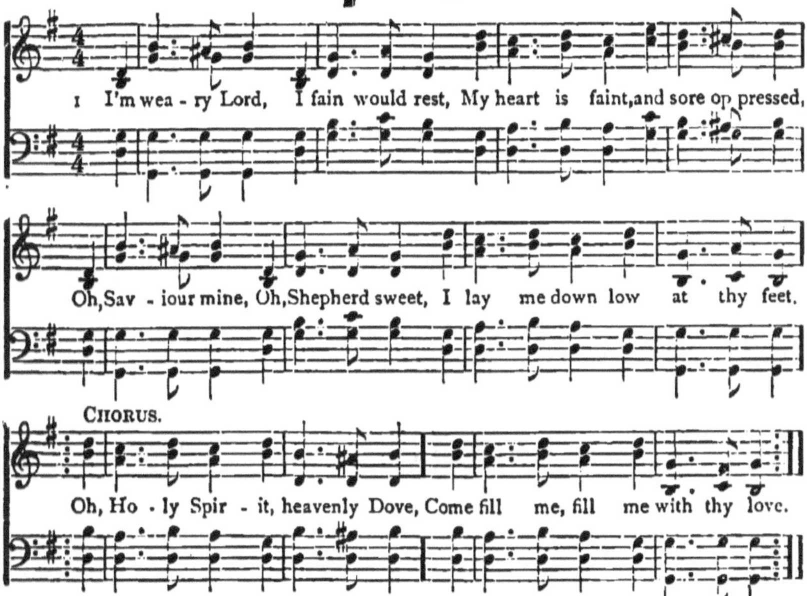

1 I'm wea-ry Lord, I fain would rest, My heart is faint, and sore op pressed,
Oh, Sav - iour mine, Oh, Shepherd sweet, I lay me down low at thy feet.

CHORUS.
Oh, Ho - ly Spir - it, heavenly Dove, Come fill me, fill me with thy love.

2 I lay me down at Mercy's throne,
Oh, seal me, Saviour, save thine own,
My all to Thee, I now resign,
Cleanse Thou my soul, sweet Master mine.

3 Long time I've prayed, and long have sought,
This priceless gift Thy blood hath bought,
Lord, take me, *make me* free from sin,
Oh, let thy fulness *now* shine in.

4 I've heard the glad triumphant shout,
Of heart made clean, of sin cast out,
Oh, mighty Father, Fount of love,
Thy glorious promise let me prove.

5 What's this that's stealing o'er my frame?
What means this holy heavenly flame?
The Lord is come, is come to me,
My cup is full, my soul is free!

Oh, Glory, Glory peace divine!
I am my Lord's and he is mine.

No. 8. **The Call.**

GEO. L. BROWN.

1. How dark and dreary, Lone and weary, Sad and sorrowful thy soul. Jesus loves you, God will save and Make thee whole. Why mourn ye? Why weep ye? Look up—'tis Jesus speaks to thee. "Come hither wayward child and rest, Oh, let the Saviour be thy guest, Oh, let the Lord of Glory in. Here at thy door I stand and knock; And lo! 'tis Satan keeps the lock—Thou'rt lost in sin."

2. Oh, leave thy sinning,
Love beginning.
Lest in this dark va': ye die.
Life awaits you,
Life and glory,
Lift thine eye.
Why wait ye?
Why doubt me?

Look up—'tis Jesus speaks to thee,
"I am the life, the way, the door,
Thy sin and all thy guilt I bore,
I paid it all on Calvary.
Except my blood hath covered thee
My Father God thou shalt not see
But thou shalt die!"

## No. 10 Believe.

By GEO. L. BROWN.

1. Oh, thou that sleep-est, rise and flee! The night comes on when none can see, Why long-er, then, the Spir-it grieve? Oh, be-lieve! be-lieve! be-lieve! Our Great High Priest hath gone on high, Where we may see him by and by, The day will soon be o-ver-past, Let us work and pray and fast.

2
He suffered once without the gate
That he might change thy sinful state;
Oh, enter now, the holy place;
Oh, be filled with love and peace;
Oh, hear him say: "Come follow me,
For thou must pure and holy be."
His own He'll ne'er forsake or leave;
Oh, believe! believe! believe!

## No. 11.
## FREE IN CHRIST.

FREDRICK WILLIAM TABOR, D.D., was a Roman Catholic priest, born in England, June 28, 1815, and died in 1863. He was a man of deep piety. The following poem describes his own conversion.

Music by G. L. BROWN.

1. There was naught in God's world half so dark or so vile As the sin and the bondage that fettered my soul; There was naught half so base as the malice and guile Of my own sordid passions, or Satan's control.

CHORUS.
But the chains that have bound me are flung to the wind By the mercy of God, the poor slave now is free; And the strong grace of heaven breathes fresh o'er my mind As the glad winds of summer sweep over the sea.

2 For years I have borne about hell in my breast,
    When I thought of my God it was nothing but gloom;
  Day brought me no pleasure, night gave me no rest,
    There was still the grim shadow of horrible doom.

3 It seemed as if nothing less likely could be
    Than that light should break in on a dungeon so deep;
  To create a new world were less hard than to free
    The slave from his bondage, the soul from its sleep.

4 But the Word had gone forth, saying: "Let there be light."
    And it flashed through my soul like a sharp, passing smart;
  One look from my Saviour, and all the dark night
    Like a dream scarce remembered, was gone from my heart.

5 I cried out for mercy and fell on my knees,
    And confessed while my heart with keen anguish was wrung;
  'Twas the labor of minutes and years of disease
    Fell as fast from my soul as the words from my tongue.

6 And now, blest be God and the dear Lord that died!
    No deer on the mountain, no bird in the sky,
  No bright wave that leaps on the dark bounding tide
    Is a creature so free or so happy as I.

## No. 12. There and Here.

GEO. L. BROWN.

*With expression.*

1. My home in heav-en, sweet home, sweet home! Oh, I would flee to thee, sweet home, sweet home,
2. Oh, land of Beu-lah, sweet rest, sweet rest, How thrills my soul in thee, sweet rest, sweet rest.

How beau-ti-ful! how beau-ti-ful! Oh, bless-ed peace! Oh, bless-ed peace

*Legato.*

Where I shall dwell e-ter-nal-ly Whene'er the Lamb of God is come, is come,
The peace of Him who cleanseth me; The peace of Him whose blood was shed for me,

*p ritard and dim.*    *pp*    CHORUS. *Lively.*

When Him we slew and crucified, is come, is come.
Whose heart we crushed, whose blood we shed upon the tree.

Oh, list the sweet music from

*Dim.*    *pp*

an-gel bands, As softly it floats to the bor-der lands, Where spirits made

# Highway Hymnal.

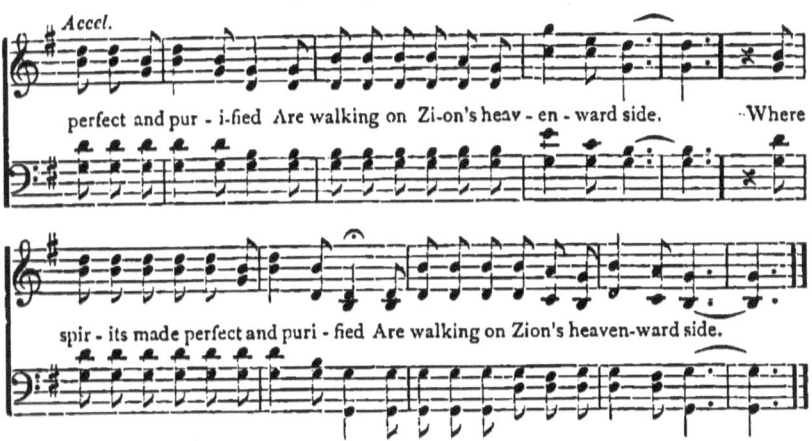

3 Oh, cross of Jesus, sweet cross, sweet cross,
Thy cross I'll bear—help me, sweet cross, sweet cross,
How light the cross of Jesus is
When borne in faith and holiness,
Whene'er His holy spirit dwells in me;
Whom we have oft and sorely grieved away, away.

4 Now keep me ever, keep me, keep me,
Close to thy bleeding side keep me, keep me.
How glorious! how glorious,
The fellowship of Jesus is.
Whene'er we're walking in His holy light,
Which we by sin once made a dark and dreary night.

## No. 13. Cross and Crown.

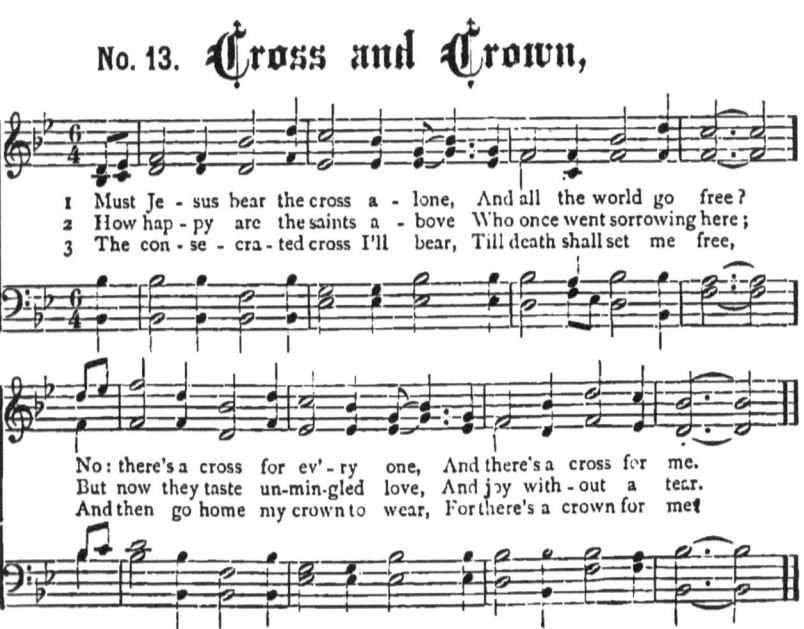

1 Must Jesus bear the cross alone, And all the world go free?
No: there's a cross for ev'ry one, And there's a cross for me.

2 How happy are the saints above Who once went sorrowing here;
But now they taste unmingled love, And joy without a tear.

3 The consecrated cross I'll bear, Till death shall set me free,
And then go home my crown to wear, For there's a crown for me!

## 14

From Holiness Songs, with per.
TUNE—"Hold the fort."

All the world is on the breakers,
Stand not idly by,
Jesus sends a call for workers,
Where can he rely?

CHO.—Glory, glory, hallelujah,
Christ hath set me free,
And my loyal soul is singing,
"Here am I, send me."

2 Everlasting woe awaits them,
'Neath the parted wave,
Who will tell the lost and dying
Christ is strong to save!

3 Hark the wreck is loudly crashing,
On the billows high,
If they hear not of the rescue,
Souls are doomed to die.

4 Who will hear the Saviour's message,
Ere the chance be o'er?
Ere the waters dark engulf them,
And they rise no more.

5 Sheltered in the Rock of Ages,
Safe from storm and sea,
All within my soul is saying,
"Here am I, send me."

6 Blood divine is freely streaming,
Cleansing in its flow,
Now to lead them to the fountain,
Jesus, I will go.

## 15

From Beulah Songs.

Jesus, Lord, I come to Thee,
Wash'd in the blood of the Lamb!
Set my longing spirit free,
Wash'd in the blood of the Lamb.

CHO.—I'm redeem'd, redeem'd,
Wash'd in the blood of the Lamb.
I'm redeem'd, redeem'd,
I am wash'd in the blood of the Lamb!

2 Speak, and let my heart be clean,
Wash'd, etc
Fully sav'd from inbred sin, Wash'd, etc.

CHO.—Redeem'd, redeem'd, etc.

3 Cleanse me, wash me white as snow,
Let me all Thy fullness know,

4 To my heart the bliss reveal,
Fix on me the Spirit's seal,

5 All thy fullness now I claim,
Through the dear Redeemer's name,

6 I am sav'd by blood divine,
All the bliss of faith is mine,

## 16

From Holiness Songs, with per.
TUNE—"Repeat the story o'er and o'er."

I walk with Jesus day by day,
Nor ever turn aside,
No Lion tracks the King's highway.
And there would I abide.

CHO.—For I am going through,
To God I will be true;
Go thro' the gates, cast up the way,
For I am going through.

2 Here God's redeemed are walking still,
In fellowship so dear,
And doing Jesus' blessed will,
Are kept from sin and fear.

3 O, let us lift the standard high,
And let it float afar;
It signals Jesus' victory,
In all this holy war.

4 'Tis trailing on the dusty sward,
O, lift it, lift it high,
Till "holiness unto the Lord,"
Shall echo through the sky..'

5 Cast out the stones, and make them room,
Prepare the people's way,
With joy the ransomed ones shall come,
And grief shall flee away,

## 17

Down at the cross where my Saviour died,
Down where for cleansing from sin I cried,
There to my heart was the blood applied,
Glory to His name.

CHO.—Glory to His name, glory to his name,
There to my heart was the blood applied,
Glory to his name.

2 I am so wondrously saved from sin,
Jesus so sweetly abides within,
Here at the cross where he took me in;
Glory to his name.

3 O precious fountain, that saves from sin;
I am so glad I have entered in;
Here Jesus saves me and keeps me clean;
Glory to his name.

4 Come to this fountain so rich and sweet;
Cast thy poor soul at the Saviour's feet;
Plunge in to-day and be made complete;
Glory to his name.
—[REVIVALIST.

## 18

From Holiness Songs, with per.
TUNE—"Jesus will help if you try."

Oh, what will it profit, my brother,
Houses and acres so broad?
No title to mansions in glory,
None to the city of God.

CHO.—What will it profit? What will it profit?
Though the whole world be thine own,
When death shall have called thee,
Thy soul lost forever,
Mercy departed and flown.

2 Oh, what will it profit, my brother,
Silver and gold for thy store,
But never hast bought of thy Saviour,
Gold that will last evermore?

3 Oh, what will it profit, my brother,
Friendships to share and to make,
And know not in friendship most precious,
One who hast died for thy sake?

4 Oh, what will it profit, my brother,
Earthly ambition and fame,
If Christ in his Life book, in glory,
Never has written thy name?

5 Oh, what will it profit, my brother,
Treasures of knowledge to hold,
And know not the God of salvation,
Know not the love still untold?

6 Oh, what will it profit, my brother,
Rivers of pleasure to have,
And never to drink of Life's river,
Never to plunge in its wave?

## No. 19.
## JESUS MAKES ME FREE INDEED.

Arranged by G. L. BROWN.

1. Now I feel the sa-cred fire Kind-ling, flam-ing, glow-ing,
   High-er ris-ing still, and higher, All my soul o'er-flow-ing;
   Life im-mor-tal I re-ceive—Oh, the won-drous sto-ry!
   I was dead, but now I live, Glo-ry! glo-ry! glo-ry!

2. Now I am from bond-age freed, Ev'-ry band is riv-en;
   Je-sus makes me free in-deed, Just as free as heav-en;
   'Tis a glo-rious lib-er-ty— Oh, the won-drous sto-ry!
   I was bound, but now I'm free, Glo-ry! glo-ry! glo-ry!

3 Let the testimony roll,
Roll through every nation,
Witnessing from soul to soul,
This immense salvation;
Now I know it's full and free,
Oh, the wondrous story!
For I feel it saving me,
Glory! glory! glory!

4 Glory be to God on high,
Glory be to Jesus,
He hath brought salvation nigh,
From all sin he frees us;
Let the golden harps of God
Ring the wondrous story;
Let the pilgrims shout aloud,
Glory! glory! glory!

## No. 20.
### STEP OUT ON THE PROMISE.
Arr. by GEO. L. BROWN.

2 O ye that are hungry and thirsty, rejoice!
For ye shall be filled—O! hear that sweet voice
Inviting you now to the banquet of God:
Step out on the promise,—get under the blood.

3 Who sighs for a heart from iniquity free?
O, poor troubled soul! there's a promise for thee;
Thou shalt rest, weary one, in the bosom of God;
Step out on the promise,—get under the blood.

4 The promise don't save, though the promise is true,
'Tis the blood we get under that cleanses us through;
It cleanses me now, O glory to God!
I rest on the promise,—I'm under the blood.

### No 21 ATONEMENT. C. M.

2 The dying thief rejoiced to see
   That fountain in his day;
And there may I, though vile as he,
   Wash all my sins away.

3 Thou dying Lamb! thy precious blood
   Shall never lose its power
Till all the ransomed church of God
   Are saved, to sin no more.

4 E'er since, by faith, I saw the stream
   Thy flowing wounds supply,
Redeeming love has been my theme,
   And shall be, till I die.

5 Then in a nobler, sweeter song,
   I'll sing thy power to save,
When this poor, lisping, stammering
   tongue
Lies silent in the grave.

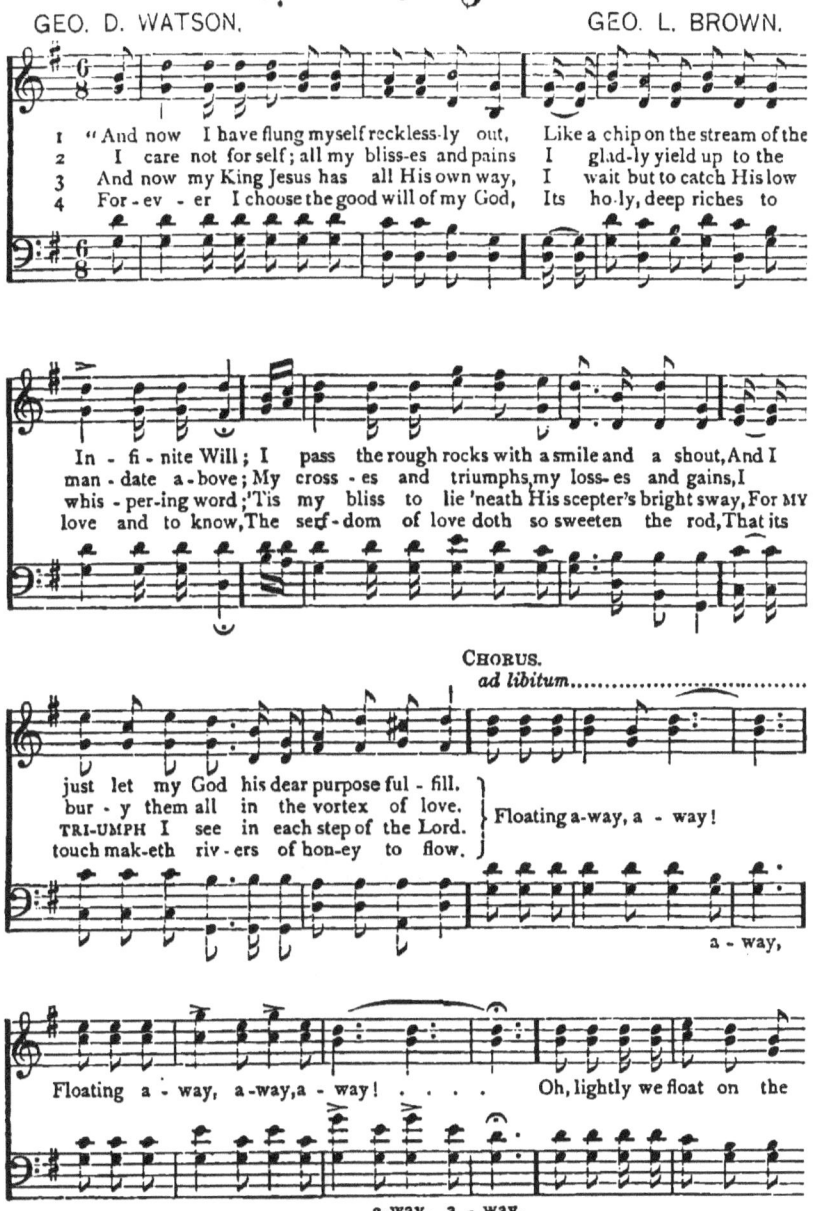

## Highway Hymnal.

o-cean of love, On the foam-crested wave-top we're floating a-way, a-way!
To the blue-vault-ed har-bor in heav-en a-bove.

5
Roll on, checkered seasons, bring smiles or bring tears,
My soul sweetly sails on an infinite tide;
I shall soon touch the shore of eternity's years,
And 'neath the white throne of my Saviour abide."

No 23 **Old Hundred. L. M.**

Praise God, from whom all blessings flow! Praise him, all creatures here be-low!
Praise him a-bove, ye heaven-ly host! Praise Father, Son, and Ho-ly Ghost!

## 24

From Holiness Songs, with per.
TUNE—"Do you hear the Saviour calling?"

Joys are flowing like a river,
  Since the Comforter has come;
He abides with us forever,
  Makes the trusting heart his home.

CHO.—Blessed quietness, holy quietness,
  What assurance in my soul,
On the stormy sea, speaking peace to me,
  How the billows cease to roll.

2 Springing into life and gladness,
  All around this glorious Guest,
Banished unbelief and sadness,
  And we just obey and rest.

3 Like the rain that falls from heaven,
  Like the sunlight from the sky,
So the Holy Ghost is given,
  Coming on us from on high.

4 See, a fruitful field is growing,
  Blessed fruits of righteousness;
And the streams of life are flowing,
  In the lonely wilderness.

5 What a wonderful salvation,
  Where we always see his face;
What a peaceful habitation,
  What a quiet resting place.

## 25

From Good Way Hymns.

Blessed assurance, Jesus is mine!
Oh, what a foretaste of glory divine!
Heir of salvation, purchased of God,
Born of His Spirit, washed in His blood.

CHO—This is my story, this is my song,
  Praising my Saviour all the day long;
This is my story, this is my song,
  Praising my Saviour all the day long.

2 Perfect salvation, perfect delight,
  Visions of rapture burst on my sight;
Angels descending, bring from above,
  Echoes of mercy, whispers of love.

3 Perfect submission, all is at rest;
  I in my Saviour am happy and blest;
Watching and waiting, looking above,
  Filled with his Spirit, lost in his love.

## 26

From the Garner.

Jesus my Lord to thee I cry,
  Unless thou help me I must die,
Oh, bring Thy free salvation nigh,
  And take me as I am!

CHO—Take me as I am, take me as I am;
  Oh, bring Thy free salvation nigh, and take me as I am!

2 Helpless I am, and full of guilt,
  But yet for me Thy blood was spilt,
And thou canst make me what Thou wilt,
  And take me as I am!

3 I thirst, I long to know Thy love,
  Thy full salvation I would prove;
But since to Thee I cannot move,
  Oh, take me as I am!

4 If Thou hast work for me to do,
  Inspire my will, my heart renew,
And work both in and by me too,
  But take me as I am!

5 And when at last the work is done,
  The battle o'er, the victory won,
Still, still my cry shall be alone,
  Oh, take me as I am!

## 27

If you get there before I do,
When the general roll is called, I'll be there;
Look out for me, I'm coming too,
When the general roll is called, I'll be there

CHORUS

I'll be there, I'll be there,
When the general roll is called, I'll be there.

2 We're pressing on to Canaan's land,
  We'll join the blood-washed pilgrim band.

3 Then we'll go up the shining way,
  We'll praise the Lord thro' endless day.

## 28

Come, ye sinners, poor and needy,
  Weak and wounded, sick and sore;
Jesus ready stands to save you,
  Full of pity, love and power,
    He is able,
  He is willing, doubt no more.

2 Now, ye needy, come and welcome,
  God's free bounty glorify;
True belief and true repentance—
  Every grace that brings you nigh—
    Without money,
  Come to Jesus Christ and buy.

3 Let not conscience make ye linger,
  Nor of fitness fondly dream;
All the fitness he requireth
  Is to feel your need of him.
    This he gives you—
  'Tis the Spirit's glimm'ring beam.

4 Come, ye weary, heavy laden,
  Bruised and mangled by the fall,
If you tarry till you're better,
  You will never come at all.
    Not the righteous—
  Sinners Jesus came to call.

5 Agonizing in the garden
  Your Redeemer prostrate lies;
On the bloody tree behold him,
  Hear him cry, before he dies,
    It is finish'd!—
  Sinners, will not this suffice?

6 Lo! th' incarnate God ascending,
  Pleads the merit of his blood:
Venture on him, venture freely;
  Let no other trust intrude:
    None but Jesus
  Can do helpless sinners good.

7 Saints and angels join in concert
  Sing the praises of the Lamb,
While the blissful seats of heaven
  Sweetly echo with his name:
    Hallelujah!
  Sinners here may do the same.

# SWING LOW, SWEET CHARIOT.

From Negro Melody.  
Arr. by GEO. L. BROWN.  
Not too fast.

1. Swing low, sweet Cha-ri-ot, Come and take me home. Swing low, sweet Chariot, Swing low, and car-ry me home. I looked o-ver Jor-dan, And lo! I there did see Angels! Angels! Come to take me home. Just be-yond the Jor-dan Jesus waits for me. Swing low! Swing low! Swing low, take me home.

2 If you get there before me,
  Just wait and watch for me;
   Angels! etc.
 Just beyond the river Jesus waits for me.
   Swing low! etc.

3 The brightest day I ever saw,
   When Jesus made me free;
    Angels! etc.
 Just across the water my Saviour waits
   Swing low! etc.  [for me.

4 He saves and keeps me ever,
   And sweetly dwells in me;
    Angels! etc.
 Just beyond the border
   He stands and beckons me.
    Swing low! etc.

5 O Sinner, come go with me,
   Bright glory waits for thee;
    Angels! etc.
 From sadness, care and sorrow
   He beckons you and me.
    Swing low! etc.

## No. 30.
## WITH GLORY IN MY SOUL.

Arr. by GEO. L. BROWN.

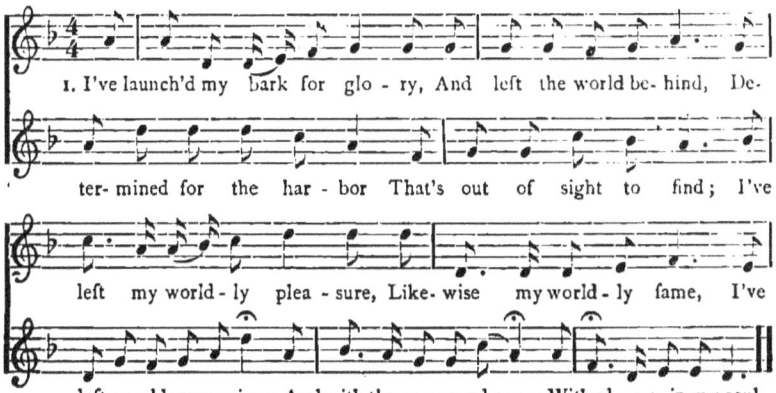

1. I've launch'd my bark for glo-ry, And left the world be-hind, De-ter-mined for the har-bor That's out of sight to find; I've left my world-ly plea-sure, Like-wise my world-ly fame, I've left my old companions, And with them my good name, With glo-ry in my soul.

2.
My sins are all forgiven,
 Which did as mountains rise,
My title clear for heaven,
 Yon country in the skies;
God's saints are my companions,
 I'm bound for endless day,
And though the storms are raging
 I'll sail along the way,
  With glory in my soul.

3.
I'm now a Christian sailor,
 One of the noisy crew,
I shout when I am happy,
 And that I mean to do;
Some say I am too noisy,
 I know the reason why,
And if they felt the glory,
 They'd shout as well as I,
  With glory in my soul.

4.
They sing and shout in heaven,
 And this is their delight;
I shout when I get happy,
 And that with all my might;
I've Jesus Christ within me,
 He's turned the devil out,
And when I feel the glory,
 It makes me sing and shout,
  With glory in my soul.

5.
Though sinners do despise us,
 And laugh at what we say,
We find a little number
 Walk with us in the way.
Come on, come on, my brethren,
 They laughed at Jesus, too;
The Kingdom is before us,
 And heaven heaves in view,
  With glory in my soul.

6.
And if I'm blamed for shouting,
 For this I do not care,
I'll urge my way to glory,
 And shout and never fear;
And when I reach the landing place,
 With those who've gone before,
Amid the blaze of glory,
 I'll shout forevermore,
  With glory in my soul.

## No. 31.
# Jubilee.
By GEO. L. BROWN.

1. Oh, glo-ry-land! Oh, ju-bi-lee! Oh, pearl-y gate! Oh, glass-y sea!
   My quick'ning vis-ion limns a scene Of sil-ver streams in fields of green.
   Oh, Beu-lah mine! Oh, ju-bi-lee! That land and song I sing and see,
   And by and bye, ye pur-i-fied, We'll shout it on the oth-er side.

2. Oh, shin-ing shore! Oh, wav-ing tree! On faith's bright wing I fly to thee;
   Thy grass-y vales and sun-bright hills, With joy-ous hope my spir-it thrills.

3. Oh, snowy robe! Oh, glory-light!
   Oh, angel forms so pure and bright!
   Oh, spirit land so fair and free,
   How throbs my heart in love to thee?

4. Oh, bought of God! Oh, blood-washed throng!
   I almost hear thy trumpet song.
   From sun to sun in thunder tone,
   "All glory to the Great White Throne!"

5. Oh, holy, Lord of Sabaoth!
   Oh, God-sent Spouse! Oh, plighted troth!
   Oh, blood-redeemed and spotless bride!
   In Thee my soul is satisfied.

No. 32.
# Tell the Story.

GEO. L. BROWN.

1. Oh, tell the story—tell it all, That all the world may know:—
"The blood of Jesus cleanseth me, And makes me white as snow."
Oh, tell the story—tell it all, And tell it o'er and o'er; Oh, tell it softly—tell it freely, "Jesus cleanseth" evermore.

2. Oh, tell the story faithfully, Nor hide a single word;
Though friends may chide, and foes may scorn, Speak on and trust the Lord.

3. Oh, tell it in humility,
To God belongs the praise;
Be strong in weakness, brave in fear,
And pure in all thy ways.

4. Oh, tell to sinner, saint, and all,
The joy of Perfect Love;—
"The Holy Spirit fills me now,
With fulness from above."

5. Not many mighty ones are called,
Not many wise and great,
Then tell it oft, ye little ones,
For soon 'twill be too late.

6. And when we reach the happy shore
Where doubt nor sin may dwell,
We'll sing the same old story o'er,
Which now we love to tell.

## 33

Oh! the wonders of creation,
And the work of nature's God,
Call for songs of admiration
As we travel life's rough road.

Cho—Who can say without blushing,
Without fear of the chastening rod,
Who can say in the light of reason,
"I believe there is no God?"

2 Behold the stars above us shining,
Sending forth their twinkling light;
And the moon is ever acting
As the police in the night.

3 Behold the sun in splendor shining,
Pouring light and warmth abroad;
Who can look upon its glory
And then say there is no God?

4 See the world in all its beauty
With its ocean's broad expanse;
See the forests and their verdure
Scattered broadcast o'er the land.

5 The world is filled with living creatures
Some are great and some are small;
And our God, the God of heaven,
Hath placed mankind over all.

6 Little streamlets from their mountain,
Pouring forth their crystal flood,
And the birdie's as they warble,—
All things tell us there's a God.

## 34

Jesus, thine all victorious love
Shed in my heart abroad;
Then shall my feet no longer rove,
Rooted and fixed in God.

2 O, that in me the sacred fire
Might now begin to glow;
Burn up the dross of base desire,
And make the mountains flow.

3 O, that it now from heaven might fall,
And all my sin consume:
Come Holy Ghost, for thee I call;
Spirit of burning, come.

4 Refining fire go through my heart,
Illuminate my soul;
Scatter thy life through every part,
And sanctify the whole.

4 My steadfast soul, from falling free,
Shall then no longer move;
While Christ is all the world to me,
And all my heart is love.

## 35

Tune—"Just Before the battle, Mother."

Jesus, Jesus, precious Jesus,
Thou art all in all to me;
I am in the cleansing fountain,
Flowing still so pure and free.
I am willing, Yes, I'm willing
To be led by thy great love,
Till I claim the golden promise,
Of a home in heaven above.

2 When I heard of thy great kindness,
And thy dying love, to save
From the world and its temptations,
And the terrors of the grave.

All my sins I took to Jesus,
Told him what I longed to claim:
Then I got the longed for promise,
Free salvation through his name.

3 Jesus, Jesus, precious Jesus,
In thy service I will die;
Fill me with thy Holy Spirit,
And then Satan I'll defy.
Come thou near me, and dwell in me,
Take and use me for thine own;
Help me by thy grace and Spirit,
Just to live for thee alone.

4 Jesus, Jesus, loving Jesus,
We are waiting now for thee;
Let us have that blessed token—
'Twas so freely shed for me,
And I know that thou canst show it,
By thy Holy Spirit's power.
Come, dear Jesus, now, and fill me,
Ever fill me from this hour.

## 36

From Holiness Songs, with per.
Tune—"What can Wash away my Sins."
Like the lillies toiling not,
Casting every care on Jesus.
Like the birds, no anxious thought,
Casting every care on Jesus.

Cho.—Oh, glorious place of rest,
No more by cares oppressed,
Leaning on Jesus' breast,
Casting every care on Jesus.

2 I have peace amid the waves, &c.
Troubles come but Jesus saves, &c.

3 Singing in the trying hour, &c.
Broken is the tempter's power, &c.

4 Trusting Him for daily bread, &c.
Soul and body both are fed, &c.

5 Burdened once, but now relieved, &c.
How it heals the spirit grieved, &c.

6 Following where ere he goes, &c.
Satisfied that Jesus knows, &c.

## 37

Am I a soldier of the cross—
A follower of the Lamb—
And shall I fear to own his cause,
Or blush to speak his name?

2 Must I be carried to the skies
On flowery beds of ease,
While others fought to win the prize,
And sailed through bloody seas?

3 Are there no foes for me to face?
Must I not stem the flood?
Is this vile world a friend to grace,
To help me on to God?

4 Since I must fight if I would reign,
Increase my courage, Lord;
I'll bear the toil, endure the pain,
Supported by thy word.

5 Thy saints in all this glorious war
Shall conquer, though they die:
They see the triumph from afar—
By faith they bring it nigh.

6 When that illustrious day shall rise,
And all thy armies shine
In robes of vict'ry through the skies,
The glory shall be thine.

## No. 38
## Clean Hands.
Job xvii: 9.

GEO. L. BROWN.

1. Let us come to the light and examine our hands, Ere we grapple the sword of the Lord;
Lest we mar all our la-bor and fail in our plans, Lest we tarnish the beautiful sword.
2. Are our fingers yet soiled with the earnings of sin? Are we eating a poor neighbor's food?
Have we chanced a sad bout with our neighbor to win? Are there left any stains of his blood?

Then wash and be clean, Oh, wash and be clean! Oh, plunge in the fountain now open for thee;
The blood of the Son, re-demption hath won, Then wash and be happy and free.

3
Have we title to lands that another man owns?
Are we hoarding another man's gold?
Do we laugh at the cost of a poor widow's groans?
When the word is: "Restore ye four-fold."

4
Has usury builded some part of our gains,
And torn a poor neighbor's barn down?
Are our pleasures made sweet by another one's pains?
Are we smiling because of his frown?

5
Let us not be deceived, for our God is not mocked;
Ever weak is the hand that's impure;
Unto such is Jehovah's great store-house e'er locked,
And their labor shall never endure.

6
By none shall the Father's bright glory be seen,
Save the holy and pure in heart;
Neither here nor in heav'n shall the soul that's unclean,
Have a share in the sweet "better part."

## No. 39.
# The Wasted Life.

Matt. xxv: 21.

GEO. L. BROWN.

2   When schemes delayed and cherished plans
    Slip from the grasp of nerveless hands;
    And hopes that lent the daily joy,
    The fainting thought no more employ;
      Then turns the mind from wasted years,
      'Tis then the long-forgotten Jesus
        Is sought in bitter tears.

3   Oh, let me not to death go down
    Beneath an angered Saviour's frown;
    But let my life, and strength of days,
    Be spent to my Redeemer's praise,
      In gathering fruit till he appears;
      'Tis then the mercy-loving Jesus
        Will wipe away my tears.

## No. 40.
## KEEP CLOSE TO THE SAVIOUR.

Arranged by GEO. L. BROWN.

1. Keep close to Jesus, And don't forget to pray,
He will cheer and guide you On the heav'nly way.

CHORUS.

Nearer, and nearer to Jesus Strive to live each day;

Keep close to the Saviour, And don't forget to pray.

2 Keep close to Jesus,
It gives the soul delight;
Soon with joy you'll greet him
On the plains of light.

3 Keep close to Jesus,
Ye weary, sorrowing one,
Let thy prayer be ever,
Lord, thy will be done.

4 Keep close to Jesus
Through rivers dark and deep,
He will light thy pathway,—
He will guide thy feet.

5 Keep close to Jesus
Until your work is done;
Till you hear the Master's
"Well done, child, come home."

## No 41
## OUR HOME IN GLORY.

I. D. SANTEE.  Music by G. L. BROWN.

1. There'll be a rift in the a-zure dome, A sight of the pearl-y gate,
D. S. And welcome us in-to par-a-dise, That land of fade-less flowers;
A sound of the trum-pet that calls us home Where angel harp-ers wait,
With shin-ing brows and lov-ing eyes, They will clasp their hands with ours,

2 That home of rest for the weary souls,
   That goal for the way-worn feet,
Where life's eternal ocean rolls,
   Where are angels harping sweet.
There are waving palms and robes of white
   Prepared by the King of heaven;
There are harps of gold and crowns of light
   For the ransomed ones forgiven.

3 Open the gates of endless day,
   The children are coming home;
An angel with each to lead the way,
   From the North and South they come;
And East and West have trumpet heard,
   And the voice of the Son of God;
The captive soul to life is stirred
   Which slumbered 'neath the sod.

HIGHWAY HYMNAL. 29

## OUR HOME IN GLORY. Concluded.

4 With joy that language can never tell
   They'll rise through the arching dome;
  For they've bid their sorrows a long farewell,—
   They are children coming home.
  And up through the nebulous, shining stars,
   They'll take their rejoicing way;
  For God himself has let down the bars,
   And opened the gates of day.

5 Finished their weary pilgrimage,
   Gone are their sighs and tears;
  The future opens its glorious page
   Through God's eternal years.
  They've reached at last a sheltering home
   Where is bliss without alloy;
  And all the redeemed to Zion come
   With everlasting joy.

6 The mold is covering many a face
   That's lying cold and low;
  But we'll clasp their forms in a warm embrace
   In that Eden home, I know.
  So I'll wait for the hour when the cloud shall rift,
   And the King of kings shall come;
  From my heart the gloom for aye shall lift
   As I rise to my heavenly home.

### No 42. THE LORD'S PRAYER.

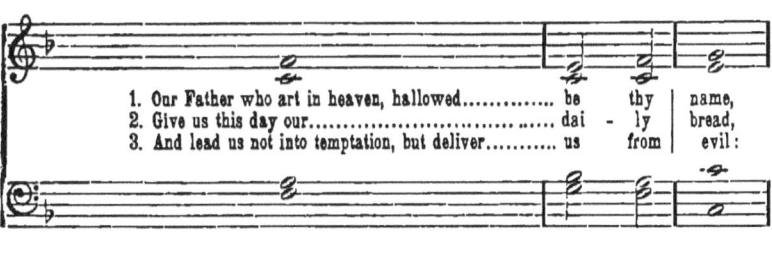

1. Our Father who art in heaven, hallowed ............... be    thy    | name,
2. Give us this day our .................................... dai  -  ly   | bread,
3. And lead us not into temptation, but deliver .......... us    from  | evil:

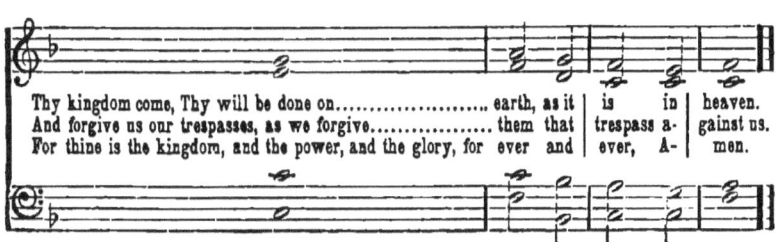

Thy kingdom come, Thy will be done on ................... earth, as it | is     in  | heaven.
And forgive us our trespasses, as we forgive .............. them that | trespass a- | gainst us.
For thine is the kingdom, and the power, and the glory, for ever and | ever,   A- | men.

## 43

From Holiness Songs, with per.
TUNE—"A Better Day is Coming."

The foxes have their dwelling,
 The little birds their nest,
But God's own Son, that blessed one,
 Had not a place of rest;
A lonely mountain pillow
 His sleeping place might be,
And kneeling there, in nightly prayer,
 His love remembered me.

CHORUS.

I will follow thee, yes, I'll follow thee,
 For Jesus and salvation, are all in all to me;
I will follow thee, yes, I will follow thee,
 Thou hast the words of endless life, I gladly follow thee.

2 A thousand tongues are calling,
 This loyal heart of mine,
And guilded toys, and fleeting joys,
 Around my pathway shine;
But, oh, they seem as nothing,
 Since Christ my heart has won;
I'll walk His ways and sing His praise,
 Till traveling days are done.

3 My shoes are brass and iron,
 On all the thorny ways,
And as I go, to meet the foe,
 My strength is as my days;
The blood of Jesus cleanseth,
 The Comforter has come;
This gentle dove has filled with love
 And made my heart his home.

4 Lo, I am with you alway,
 I hear the promise ring,
He holds my hand in ev'ry land,
 I journey with the King;
He gives me grace and glory,
 He is my sun and shield,
I'll feed His sheep, for Him I'll reap,
 The whitening harvest field.

## 44

From Holiness Songs, with per.
TUNE—"Will your Anchor hold in the Storms of Life."

In the temple old with its holy shrine,
With its burnished gold and light divine,
Were the figures true of the coming One,
When the old things new had all become.

CHORUS

We have an Altar 'tis Christ divine,
Cleansing from sin this glad heart of mine,
Resting here by faith will I abide,
And the Spirit saith I am sanctified.

2 Now the shadows dim having passed away,
Let us look to Him who brings the day,
For the light has come and the Lord is here,
Sing aloud ye dumb, with faith draw near.

3 In the streaming blood of that temple old,
How the Lamb of God was plain foretold,
And the Altar shrine where such virtue lies
Was the Lord divine who sanctifies.

4 So my offering free to my Lord I bring,
All there is of me to serve the King.
Blessed Holy Ghost, how He fills my heart,
With the blood-washed host gives me apart.

5 When my all was given and 'twas all complete,
Swiftly came from heaven the witness sweet,
And the Spirit's power helps me touch by faith,
And the gift is pure, as Jesus saith.

## 45

From "Songs of Triumph." By per.

I am sav'd! the Lord hath sav'd me,
 Help me shout the glorious news!
I have tasted God's salvation,
 And 'tis sweet as honeyed dews.

CHO—Glory, glory, hallelujah,
 I rejoice, salvation came;
 Glory, glory, hallelujah!
 I am saved in Jesus' name.

2 Loud I sing my exultation,
 Hoping it will reach the skies,
Keep, dear Lord, my soul forever
 Under Thy protecting eyes.

3 Free salvation! glad salvation!
 Let us shout from pole to pole,
Until each diseased nation
 Feels that God hath made it whole.

4 When at last the days are gathered,
 Into Thy great judgment one,
May I find my name deep written
 In the records of Thy Son.

## 46

From "Songs of Triumph." By per.

When the voyage of life is ended,
 And the stormy winds shall cease,
When we step from care and sorrow,
 To eternal joy and peace.

CHO—Hallelujah! hallelujah! what a meeting!
 But the best of all will be,
 Our Redeemer, dear Redeemer,
 In his beauty we shall see.

2 When we gather in the morning,
 And the long, long night is o'er,
When we clasp our hands united,
 And our partings come no more.

3 O, the pearly gates of glory,
 Not ajar, but open wide,
Even now our faith behold them,
 As we near the swelling tide.

4 Hallelujah! hallelujah!
 O, ye ransomed hosts above,
We are coming, we are coming,
 Soon we'll join your songs of love.

## 47

From "Songs of Triumph." By per.

I'm saved! I'm saved! oh, blessed Lord,
 I'm sweetly saved in Thee,
Saved by Thy blood, and by Thy word,
 And thine henceforth will be.

CHO—I'm saved! I'm saved! I'm saved!
 I'm washed in the blood of the Lamb!
 I'm saved! I'm saved! I'm saved!
 I'm washed in the blood of the Lamb.

2 I'm saved, I'm saved! oh, joy sublime!
 I'm saved from self and sin,
I'm saved, I'm saved, oh, bliss divine!
 And love has closed me in.

3 Saved at the cross, the blessed cross,
 Saved without and within,
I'm saved, I'm saved, oh what a loss,
 Who fail this joy to win.

4 I'm saved, I'm saved, I'll tell it here,
 I'll sing it o'er and o'er,
I'm saved in Jesus, oh, how sweet!
 I'll sing it evermore.

**No. 48.**
## There'll be rest By and Bye.

G. L. B.          GEO. L. BROWN.

2
There'll be rest by and bye
For the care-encumbered heart,
There'll be rest from the toil and bitter strife;
And nor anguish nor death,
Nor the sting of envy's dart,
Shall have place in that sweet better life.

3
There'll be rest by and bye
For the traveller bowed with years,
There'll be rest for the pilgrim faint and sore;
For His angels are near
Who will wipe away all tears,
And we'll dwell in His light evermore.

## No. 49.
## PILGRIM'S BEULAH.

*Get the Experience.*          Music by GEO. L. BROWN.

1. Bright scenes of glo-ry strike my sense, And all my pas-sions capture,
2. I feast on hon-ey, milk and wine, I drink per-pet-ual sweetness;
3. My footsteps trace the pleasant meads And myrtle fields of o-dor,

E-ter-nal beau-ties round me shine, In-fus-ing warm-est rap-ture.
Mt. Zi-on yields her rich per-fumes, While Christ unfolds His greatness.
While groves of spice my noonday shade, And spread in rich-est grandeur.

I dive in o-ceans deep and full, That swell in waves of glo-ry;
No mor-tal tongue can tell my joys, Nor can an an-gel show them—
The chant of ser-aphs lifts my soul Till caught with heaven-ly fire,

I feel the Sav-iour in my soul, And long to tell the sto-ry.
Ten thousand times sur-pass-ing all Ter-res-tial words or emblems.
And love di-vine to me un-folds, And tunes my heart the high-er.

4 My captivated spirit flies
  Through worlds of shining beauty;
Dissolved in love, to heaven I cry
  In praises loud and mighty.
I here eternal notes employ
  In songs of rapturous glory,
O'erwhelming all my powers with joy
  With free salvation's story.

5 When earth and sea shall be no more,
  And all their glory perish,
When sun and moon shall cease to shine,
  And stars at midnight languish,
I then shall rise and soar away—
  Mount heaven's radiant glory—
And tell, through one eternal day,
  Love's all immortal story.

## No. 50
## The Shining Way.

G. L. B.  Text—Prov. iv. 18.  Geo. L. Brown.

1. There is a realm that's bright and fair,—I see its gleaming por-tals;
2. A light that shin-eth more and more,—So runs the bles-sed sto-ry,
3. I am the Light,—so Je-sus said,—I am the Lamp that's given,

A shining way leads o-ver there, A light for dy-ing mor-tals.
From Egypt's land to Canaan's shore, From sin's dark night to glo-ry.
Which, if thine eye is on me stayed, Will guide thy soul to heav-en.

REFRAIN.

My feet are on the shin-ing way, Then let the mu-sic roll;
I'm hast'ning to the Per-fect Day, I'm hap-py in my soul.

4 Why longer wander in the night
The cold, bleak way infernal?
Just o'er the line 'tis warm and bright,
I know its joys supernal.

5 I know, I know,—oh, rapture sweet,
I know its blessed seeming;
I'm walking on the shining street,
Of heaven my soul is dreaming.

## 51

Come, ye that love the Lord,
 And let your joys be known:
Join in a song with sweet accord,
 While ye surround the throne,
Let those refuse to sing
 Who never knew our God;
But servants of the heavenly King
 May speak their joys abroad.

2 The God that rules on high,
 That all the earth surveys,
That rides upon the stormy sky,
 And calms the roaring seas;
This mighty God is ours,
 Our Father and our love;
He will send down his heavenly powers
 To carry us above.

3 The men of grace have found
 Glory begun below:
Celestial fruit on earthly ground
 From faith and hope my grow:
Then let our songs abound,
 And every tear be dry;
We're marching thro' Immanuel's ground
 To fairer worlds on high.

## 52

I love thy kingdom, Lord,
 The house of thine abode,
The Church our blest Redeemer saved
 With his own precious blood.

2 I love thy Church, O God!
 Her walls before thee stand,
Dear as the apple of thine eye,
 And graven on thy hand.

3 For her my tears shall fall;
 For her my prayers ascend;
To her my care and toils be given,
 Till toils and cares shall end.

4 Beyond my highest joys
 I prize her heavenly ways;
Her sweet communion, solemn vows,
 Her hymns of love and praise.

5 Sure as thy truth shall last,
 To Zion shall be given
The brightest glories earth can yield,
 And brighter bliss of heaven.

## 53

From "Songs of Triumph," with per.

'Tis so sweet to trust in Jesus,
 Just to take Him at his word;
Just to rest upon his promise;
 Just to know "Thus saith the Lord."

Cho—Jesus, Jesus, how I trust him:
 How I've proved him o'er and o'er,
Jesus, Jesus, precious Jesus!
 O for grace to trust Him more.

2 O how sweet to trust in Jesus,
 Just to trust His cleansing blood;
Just in simple faith to plunge me
 'Neath the healing, cleansing flood.

3 Yes, 'tis sweet to trust in Jesus,
 Just from sin and self to cease;
Just from Jesus simply taking,
 Life, and rest, and joy, and peace.

4 I'm so glad I learn'd to trust Thee,
 Precious Jesus, Saviour, Friend,
And I know that thou art with me,
 Wilt be with me to the end.

## 54

From Holiness Songs, with per.
Tune—"Shall we Gather at the River?"

Thirsty soul, the Lord is calling,
 Where the living waters flow;
Hear the blessed accents falling,
 To the cleansing fountain go.

Chorus.

Yes, I am drinking at the fountain,
 The wonderful, the wonderful fountain;
Drinking at the life-giving fountain
 That's flowing so full and free.

2 Through the desert, dry and dreary,
 See the glorious waters roll;
Thirsty one, so faint and weary,
 Come and satisfy thy soul.

3 Broken cisterns gladly leaving,
 To the fount of life I came;
Full salvation here receiving,
 In the all-atoning Lamb.

4 Once I drank of earthly pleasure,
 Drifted with the moving tide;
Now I'm drinking without measure,
 And am fully satisfied.

5 Like the sea its fullness bringing,
 Like a river grand and free,
Like a fountain ever springing
 Is the Comforter to me.

## 55

From Winnowed Hymns.

Will you go, brother, go
 To the highlands of heaven?
Where the storms never blow,
 And the long summer's given;
Where no fear nor dismay,
 Neither trouble nor sorrow,
Will be felt for to-day,
 Nor be feared for the morrow.

Cho—O, come, brother, come!
 While your Lord is entreating,
For the Saviour will soon
 And forever cease pleading.

2 He's prepared thee a home,—
 Brother, wilt thou believe it?
And invites thee to come;
 Sister, wilt thou receive it?
Where the saints robed in white—
 Cleansed in life's flowing fountain,
Shining beauteous and bright,
 They inhabit the mountain.

3 Will you go to that land,
 Where your friends wait to greet you?
There a beautiful band
 Join with us to entreat you;
They are waiting above—
 Waiting happy to hail you,
In that region of love
 Where no ill can assail you.

## No. 57.
## KEEP ME NEAR THE CROSS.

B. F. BLAKELY.                  GEO. L. BROWN.

1. O God! my heart doth cry to Thee, Keep me near the cross;
Though men and de-mons trou-ble me; Keep me near the cross;
My time, my tal-ents all are Thine, My hands, my feet and tho'ts combined; O

2. I can-not stand on earth a-lone, Keep me near the cross;
*D.S.* set the seal of love Di-vine! Keep me near the cross;
*D.S.* For grace Di-vine I make my moan, Keep me near the cross,
*D.S.* -rect my steps while here be-low,— Keep me near the cross;
O Lord, my God, come quickly now, My heart is full, I've seal'd my vow,—Di-

3 While wicked men do seek my life,
   Keep me near the cross;
Give me Thy strength, it will suffice,
   Keep me near the cross;
O Lord, I know Thy strength is great!
Though sudden death should be my fate,—
O let me now Thy light partake!
   Keep me near the cross.

4 I know Thy work I must perform,
   Keep me near the cross;
Though all be calm or raging storm,
   Keep me near the cross;
But Thou, my Lord, must give the field,
The sword, the staff, the mighty shield,—
And then the hearts of men must yield,
   Keep me near the cross.

5 I know, Great God, this means so much,
   Keep me near the cross;
That I should bear the world's reproach,
   Keep me near the cross;
O Lord, my Lord, how can it be
That Thou shouldst call a worm like me?
For grace Divine I call to Thee,
   Keep me near the cross.

## 58

Tune—"O, Thou God of my Salvation."

O my God, how thy salvation
  Fills my soul with peace and joy,
Patience gives, and consolation
  Which the world cannot destroy!
    Full salvation!
  Which the world cannot destroy.

2 For that love whose tender mercies
    Purest joys do daily bring,
  I will in my life confess thee,
    With my mouth thy praises sing:
      Full salvation!
    With my mouth thy praises sing.

3 Full salvation! Full salvation!
    Lo! the fountain opened wide,
  Streams through every land and nation
    From the Saviour's wounded side.
      Full salvation!
    Streams an endless crimson tide.

4 Oh! the glorious revelation!
    See the cleansing current flow,
  Washing stains of condemnation
    Whiter than the driven snow;
      Full salvation!
    Oh, the rapturous bliss to know!

5 Love's resistless current sweeping
    All the regions deep within:
  Thought, and wish, and senses keeping
    Now, and every instant, clean;
      Full salvation!
    From the guilt and power of sin.

6 Life immortal, heaven descending,
    Lo! my heart's the Spirit's shrine!
  God and man in oneness blending—
    Oh, what fellowship is mine!
      Full salvation!
    Raised in Christ in life divine!

7 Praise to God, the glorious giver,
    Christ the Saviour of the lost,
  And the Comforter forever,
    Father, Son, and Holy Ghost!
      Full salvation!
    Father, Son, and Holy Ghost.

## 59

2 The dying thief rejoiced to see
    That fountain in his day;
  And there have I, though vile as he,
    Washed all my sins away.

3 Dear dying Lamb, thy precious blood
    Shall never lose its power,
  Till all the ransomed Church of God
    Are saved, to sin no more.

4 E'er since by faith I saw the stream
    Thy flowing wounds supply,
  Redeeming love has been my theme,
    And shall be till I die.

5 Then, in a nobler, sweeter song,
    I'll sing thy power to save,
  When this poor lisping, stam'ring tongue,
    Lies silent in the grave.—[Cowper.

## 60

The cross! the cross! the blood-stained cross!
  The hallow'd cross I see,
Reminding me of precious blood
  That once was shed for me.

CHORUS.

Oh the blood! the precious blood! that Jesus shed for me
Upon the cross in crimson flood, just now by faith I see.

2 A thousand thousand fountains spring
  Up from the throne of God;
  But none to me such blessings bring
    As Jesus' precious blood.

3 That priceless blood my ransom paid
    While I in bondage stood;
  On Jesus all my sins were laid;
    He saved me with his blood.

4 By faith that blood now sweeps away
    My sins, as like a flood;
  Nor lets one guilty blemish stay;
    All praise to Jesus' blood!

5 This wondrous theme will best employ
    My harp before my God;
  And make all heaven resound with joy
    For Jesus' cleansing blood.—[McDonald.

## 61

O, now I see the crimson wave,
  The fountain deep and wide,
Jesus, my Lord, mighty to save,
  Points to his wounded side.

Cho—The cleansing stream, I see, I see,
  I plunge, and O, it cleanseth me,
  O, praise the Lord, it cleanseth me,
  It cleanseth me, yes cleanseth me.

2 I see the new creation rise,
  I hear the speaking blood,
It speaks, polluted nature dies,
  Sinks 'neath the cleansing flood.

3 I rise to walk in heaven's own light,
  Above the world and sin,
With heart made pure and garments white
  And Christ enthroned within.

4 Amazing grace, 'tis heaven below,
  To feel the blood applied,
And Jesus, only Jesus know,
  My Jesus crucified.—Phœbe Palmer.

## 62

From "Songs of Triumph."

O sinner, come along with me,
  I'm going home to glory;
The blood of Jesus set you free,
  I'm going home to glory.

Ref—I'm going home, I'm going home,
  I'm going home to die no more,
  I'm going home to glory;
  I'm going home, I'm going home,
  I'm going home to die no more,
  I'm going home to glory.

2 The world can charm my soul no more,
  I'm bound to reach the heavenly shore.

3 I've left my sins behind the cross,
  All earthly things I count but loss.

4 I'm ransomed from the fearful fall,
  And Jesus is my all in all.

## No. 64.
## The Heavenly Treasure.

THE writer, in 1878, was called upon to write the will of an old miner; after the will had been written the miner called his only son to his side, presented the family Bible to him, and said he had found richer treasure in the Bible than he ever had in a mine.

Words by J. R. WILLIAMS.   Music by GEO. L. BROWN.

1. Come, sit down here be-side me, A sto-ry I'll un-fold,
2. Come, tell me if you love him, Love him with all your heart,
3. Come, calm-ly think it o-ver, For to the sin-ful heart

'Tis All a-bout the Saviour's love, As in the Bi-ble told:
For if you do he'll nev-er say, From Me you must de-part!
On the e-ter-nal judgment day He'll say, Depart, de-part!

The gold-en, gold-en streets above Resound with Je-sus' love;
Come, take this Bi-ble with you, And read it o'er and o'er,
Come, for the sad-dest mes-sage Un-to the hu-man heart,

*ad lib.*

The gold-en, gold-en streets a-bove Ech-o his pre-cious love.
For nev-er was a mine so full Of rich-est gold-en ore.
Will be to hear the Sav-iour say, From Me depart, de-part!

2 But if a branch be barren,
　The Husbandman appears
And casts it in the oven,
　Among the chaff and tares;
And there in outer darkness
　The fruitless soul may dwell
Among the fallen spirits
　Whom God thrust down to hell.

3 But if a little fruitage,
　Among thy leaves appears,
His perfect love will fill thee,
　And banish all thy fears,
Then, flourishing in beauty,
　Thy fruit shall multiply,
And at the last be planted
　In Glory's realm on high.

4 Ye dwellers in our Zion,
　Of God the Spirit born,
Where are your purple clusters
　To greet the Golden Morn?
For if the bough be fruitless
　The Pruner's polished blade
Shall cleave thy soul asunder
　Who hath the Son betrayed.

5 Now, blessed Lord and Master,
　Ascends my song to thee,
For that thy Spirit Holy
　From sin hath set me free;
All hail the blood that purgeth,
　All hail the Christ of God,
In whom my soul abideth,
　Close by the chast'ning rod.

## 66
From "Welcome Tidings."

What can wash away my sins,
Nothing but the blood of Jesus;
What can make me whole again?
Nothing but the blood of Jesus.

Cho—Oh, precious is the flow
That makes me white as snow,
No other fount I know,
Nothing but the blood of Jesus.

2 For my cleansing this I see—
For my pardon this my plea—

3 Nothing can for sin atone,
Naught of good that I have done.

4 This is all my hope and peace—
This is all my righteousness.

## 67
Reprint from "The Highway."

What subdued and conquered me?
Nothing but the blood of Jesus.
What first set my spirit free?
Nothing but the blood of Jesus.

Cho—O, precious, &c.

2 What has sanctified my soul?
What has made my spirit whole?

3 What now saves me from all sin?
What now keeps me pure within?

4 What gives victory day by day?
What gives joy through all the way?

## 68
Old Song Book. [See Tune 20]

The Lord is the fountain of goodness and love:
In Eden once flowing, in streams from above,
Refreshed, every moment, the first happy pair,
Till sin stopped the torrent and brought in despair.

2 O wretched condition—what anguish and pain;
They thirst for the fountain, but seek it in vain;
To sin's bitter waters they fly for relief;
They drink, but the draught still increases their grief.

3 Glad tidings! glad tidings! no more we'll complain,
Our Jesus has opened the fountain again.
Now mingled with mercy and rich with free grace
From Zion 'tis flowing for all the lost race.

4 How happy thy prospect, how pleasant the road,
When led down the stream by the Spirit of God;
Though shallow at first, yet we find it at last
A river, so boundless, it cannot be passed.

5 Come, Christians, and venture along down the stream,
The shallows are pleasing, but O let us swim:
Let us bathe in the ocean of infinite love;
Let us wash and be pure as the angels above.

## 69
Christ was born in Bethlehem,
And in a manger laid,
Christ was born in Bethlehem,
And in a manger laid,
Christ was born in Bethlehem
And in a manger laid,
And the Lord will call his children home.

Chorus.
He arose, He arose, He arose from the dead,
He arose, He arose, He arose from the dead,
He arose, He arose, He arose from the dead,
And the Lord will call His children home.

2 'Tis the very same Jesus,
The Jews crucified.

3 One Joseph begged his body
And laid it in the tomb.

4 The grave it could not hold him,
For he was the Son of God.

5 Down came a mighty angel,
And rolled away the stone.

6 The earth began to tremble,
The Roman soldiers fell.

7 Poor Mary came a weeping,
And looking for her Lord.

8 Two men in shining raiment,
They sat within the tomb.

9 O, where now have you laid him?
He's not within the Tomb.

10 Go tell to John and Peter,
Their Jesus lives again,
That he rose, etc.

11 But he said he'd come again,
And take his people home,
For he rose, etc.

12 Shout, shout the victory,
We're on our journey home.

## 70
Copyright by Rev. L. Hartsough. With per.

How bright the hope that Calvary brings,
Where love divine with mercy blends,
How full the joy that all may find,
Where flows the blood can save and cleanse.

Cho—I am glad there is cleansing in the blood,
I am glad there is cleansing in the blood,
Tell the world, all the world,
There is cleansing in the Saviour's blood.

2 'Tis there, 'tis there the soul may go,
And wash its sins and stains away,
Who gives up all, who comes by faith,
This cleansing finds without delay.

3 Speak, speak to Zion's burdened ones,
Lead, lead them up to Calvary's mount;
The want of aching hearts is met,
'Tis cleansing in redemption's fount.

4 Why need we struggle on in self,
We cannot make one black spot white;
'Tis Christ's own blood and that alone,
Can change and cleanse the heart aright.

5 I come! I come! and glad I am
That Jesus calls the lost and vile;
There thousands have a cleansing found,
I'll heed the Saviour's welcome smile.

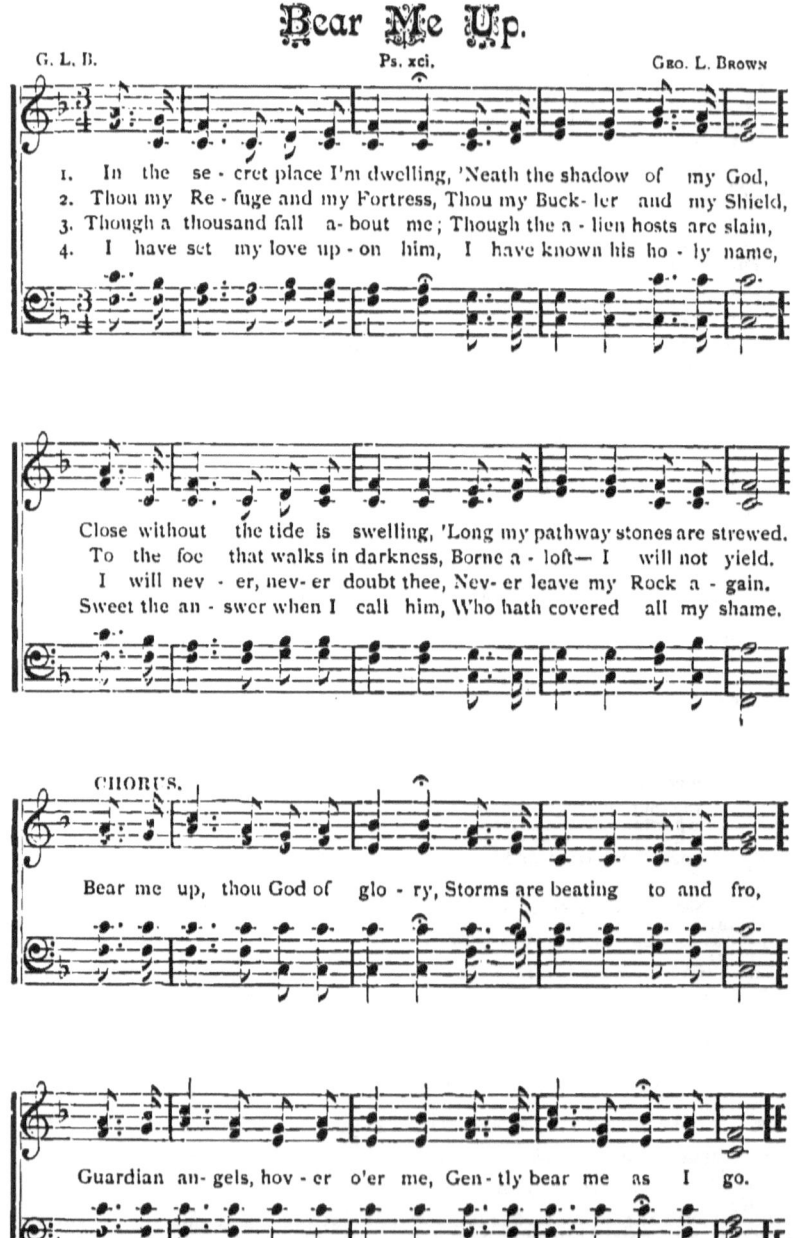

## No. 72
## BURN IT OUT.

"He shall sit as a refiner and purifier."—MAL. iii, 3.

GEO. L. BROWN.

1. If there's an-y self in me, Burn it out, burn it out;
2. If there's pride with-in my heart, Burn it out, burn it out;
3. If there's en-vy in my soul, Burn it out, burn it out;

If there's aught that's un-like Thee, Burn it out, burn it out.
Bid it far from me de-part, Burn it out, burn it out.
Make and keep my spir-it whole, Burn it out, burn it out.

CHORUS.
Ho-ly Spir-it, fall on me, Cleanse me now, cleanse me now;
From the sin-dross set me free, Burn it out, burn it out.

4 If there's bitterness and wrath,
   Burn it out, burn it out;
'Twill defile the narrow path,
   Burn it out, burn it out.

5 Does my spirit scold and fret,
   Burn it out, burn it out;
Do I murmur and dispute,
   Burn it out, burn it out.

6 If there's longing for display,
   Burn it out, burn it out;
For apparel rich and gay,
   Burn it out, burn it out.

7 Is the carnal mind within,
   Burn it out, burn it out;
Does the "old man's" form remain,
   Burn it out, burn it out.

## No. 73.
# THE CHRISTIAN'S HOPE OF HEAVEN.

GEO. L. BROWN.

1. I'm seek-ing a home in the beau-ti-ful cit-y Where all the bright years of e-ter-ni-ty roll, For-ev-er and ev-er in Glo-ry I'll be; There's a glad hope of hea-ven way down in my soul, There's a glad hope of heaven way down in my soul.

2. What strains of sweet mu-sic fall low on my ear In tones so de-light-ful, oh, list! that ye hear: Those rich flow-ing notes; oh, how sweet and how clear, Breathe the rap-ture un-told from some hea-ven-ly sphere, Breathe the rapture un-told from some heaven-ly sphere.

3. 'Tis the sweet flowing mu-sic that steals o'er the wave Of Jor-dan's lone riv-er, whose bil-lows I brave; 'Tis the mu-sic of an-gels who hast-en to bear My soul o'er the wa-ters to that bless-ed shore, My soul o'er the wa-ters to that bless-ed shore.

4. A glimpse of bright glo-ry now beams on my sight, I sink in sweet vis-ions of heav'n's dawn-ing light; Bright spir-its are whisp'ring so soft in my ear Of hea-ven, sweet heaven! I long to be there, Of hea-ven, sweet heaven! I long to be there.

## No. 74.
## NEAR THE CROSS.

GEO. L. BROWN.  Arr. by G. L. B.

1. Near the cross where Jesus found me, Long time ago;
2. Then He gave His Holy spirit Long time ago;
3. Mingled were our hearts together, Long time ago;

Oh, what glory shone around me, Bright, bright the glow.
Spotless robe—He bade me wear it—Whiter than snow.
Can I now forget Him? Never! No, Saviour, no!

All the idols I had cherished Christ bade them go,
Cleansing now and sanctifying Where'er I go,
Since my Lord has sweetly taught me Love's spell to know,

Thro' His pow'r they quickly perished, Long time ago.
Ev'ry day His blood applying, Precious the flow.
Since His precious blood has bought me, With Him I'll go.

## 75

*From "Spiritual Songs."*

Have you been to Jesus for the cleansing power,
Are you washed in the blood of the Lamb;
Are you fully trusting in His grace this hour,
Are you washed in the blood of the Lamb?

Cho—Are you washed in the blood,
 In the soul-cleansing blood of the Lamb?
 Are your garments spotless, are they white as snow,
 Are you washed in the blood of the Lamb?

2 Are you walking daily by the Saviour's side,
Are you washed in the blood of the Lamb;
Do you rest each moment in the Crucified,
Are you washed in the blood of the Lamb?

3 When the bridegroom cometh will your robes be white,
Pure and white in the blood of the Lamb;
Will your soul be ready for the mansions bright,
And be washed in the blood of the Lamb?

4 Lay aside the garments that are stained with sin,
And be washed in the blood of the Lamb;
There's a fountain flowing for the soul unclean,
O, be washed in the blood of the Lamb!

## 76

*From "Holiness Hymnal."*

Let us sing of his love once again,
Of the love that never can decay,
Of the blood of the Lamb newly slain,
Till we praise Him again in that day.

Cho—I believe—Jesus saves,
 And His blood makes me "whiter than snow."

2 There is cleansing and healing for all
Who will wash in the life-giving flood;
There is a life everlasting and joy
At the right-hand of God through the blood.

3 Even now while we taste of His love
We are filled with delight at His name;
But what will it be when above
We shall join in the song of the Lamb.

4 Then we'll march in His name till we come
At His bidding to enter our rest;
And the Father shall welcome us home
To our place in the realms of the blest.

5 So with banner unfurled to the breeze,
Our motto shall holiness be,
Till the crown at His feet we shall seize,
And the King in His glory we see.

## 77

All hail the power of Jesus' name!
Let angels prostrate fall;
Bring forth the royal diadem,
And crown him Lord of all.

2 Ye chosen seed of Israel's race,
Ye ransom'd from the fall,
Hail him who saves you by his grace,
And crown Him Lord of all.

3 Sinners, whose love can ne'er forget
The wormwood and the gall,
Go, spread your trophies at his feet,
And crown him Lord of all.

4 Let every kindred, every tribe,
On this terrestrial ball,
To him all majesty ascribe,
And crown him Lord of all.

5 O! that with yonder sacred throng,
I at his feet may fall,
And join the everlasting song,
And crown him Lord of all.—[Perronet.

## 78

*From "Precious Songs."*

With earth's adoring throng, with spirits glorified,
My soul would join the song, of Jesus crucified.
Of Jesus crucified, of Jesus crucified,
My soul would join the song, of Jesus crucified.

2 When in the hour of grief, my soul for pardon cried,
What brought me sweet relief? 'Twas Jesus crucified,
'Twas Jesus crucified, 'Twas Jesus crucified,
What brought me sweet relief? 'Twas Jesus crucified.

3 When cares and doubts oppress, when faith and hope are tried,
I turn for joy and peace, to Jesus crucified.
To Jesus crucified, to Jesus crucified;
I turn for joy and peace, to Jesus crucified.

4 Though joy may ebb and flow with fluctuating tide,
My peace no change shall know in Jesus crucified.
In Jesus crucified, in Jesus crucified;
My peace no change shall know, in Jesus crucified.

5 I seek no other bliss, no other hope beside,
No other plea than this—my Jesus crucified.
My Jesus crucified, my Jesus crucified;
No other plea than this, my Jesus crucified.

## 79

*From "Songs of Triumph."*

Behold the ark of God,
Behold the open door,
O, haste to gain that blest abode,
And rove my soul no more.

Ref—O come, come to-day, do not longer delay,
 The ark, precious bark, floateth by;
 The waves as they roll, Shall not cover thy soul,
 For Jesus, thy Saviour, is nigh.

2 There safe shalt thou abide;
There sweet shall be thy rest;
And ev'ry wish be satisfied,
With full salvation blest.

3 And when the waves of wrath
Again the earth shall fill,
Thine ark shall ride the sea of fire,
And rest on Zion's hill.

No. 80  47
# THE SHEPHERD'S GENTLE CALL.

MAGGIE E. STAMBAUGH.  Music by GEO. L. BROWN

1. The Shepherd is tenderly calling thee now, Oh, lost one, He's calling for thee;
The ninety and nine He's left in the fold, And now He is seeking for thee.

CHORUS.
Lost one, the Shepherd is call-ing, Call-ing for thee; Accept the sweet ref-uge He offers you now, Oh, lost one, He's calling for thee!

2. Too far you have wandered away from the fold,
   Till deep in the dark mire of sin,
   He's calling you back to the bright gates of gold,
   Oh, lost one, now come unto Him!

3. Your loved ones are pleading, the Saviour to save
   The lost one that's gone from the fold;
   The angels are waiting with wide-open arms
   To receive you with joy never told.

4. The ninety and nine will welcome you back,
   And give you a place in the fold;
   The Shepherd has said: "thou never shalt lack!"
   O seek the bright City of Gold.

5. Oh, lost one, now hearken to Jesus' sweet voice,
   So tenderly calling thee in!
   The voice of your God who now will rejoice
   To save you from self and from sin.

## 81

☞ *Please sing as Revised.*

Arise my soul, arise;
Though thou art justified,
Thy Saviour bids thee yet
  lie wholly sanctified.
Before the throne my surety stands,
My name is written on his hands.

2 He ever lives above,
   For me to intercede;
  His all redeeming love,
   His precious blood to plead;
  His blood atoned for all our race,
  And sprinkles now the throne of grace.

3 Five bleeding wounds he bears,
   Received on Calvary,
  They pour effectual prayers,
   They strongly plead for me:
  "Forgive him, O, forgive," they cry;
  "Nor let that ransomed sinner die."

4 The Father hears Him pray,
   His dear anointed One;
  He cannot turn away
   The presence of His Son:
  His Spirit answers to the blood,
  And tells me I am born of God.

5 My God is reconciled;
   His pardoning voice I hear;
  He owns me for His child,
   I can no longer fear:
  With confidence I now draw nigh,
  And "Father, Abba, Father," cry.

## 82
*From The "Revivalist."*

In some way or other, "the Lord will provide;"
It may not be my way, it may not be thy way,
And yet in His own way, "the Lord will provide."

2 At some time or other, 'the Lord will provide;"
It may not be my time, it may not be thy time,
And yet in His own time, "the Lord will provide."

3 Despond, then, no longer, "the Lord will provide;"
And this be the token, no word he hath spoken
Was ever yet broken; "the Lord will provide."

4 March on, then, right boldly; the sea shall divide;
The pathway made glorious with shoutings victorious,
We'll join in the chorus, "the Lord will provide."

## 83

A charge to keep I have
A God to glorify;
A never dying soul to save,
And fit it for the sky.

2 To serve the present age,
   My calling to fulfill,—
  O, may it all my powers engage,
   To do my Master' will.

3 Arm me with jealous care,
   As in Thy sight to live;
  And O, Thy servant, Lord, prepare,
   A strict account to give.

4 Help me to watch and pray,
   And on Thyself rely,
  Assured, if I my trust betray,
   I shall forever die.

## 84

My soul be on thy guard;
Ten thousand foes arise;
The hosts of sin are pressing hard
To draw thee from the skies.

2 O, watch and fight and pray;
  The battle ne'er give o'er;
  Renew it boldly every day,
  And help divine implore!

3 Ne'er think the victory won,
  Nor lay thine armor down;
  The work of faith will not be done
  Till thou obtain the crown.

4 Then persevere till death
  Shall bring thee to thy God;
  He'll take thee at thy parting breath
  To his divine abode.

## 85

The world is overcome by the blood of the Lamb,
  Glory to the Lamb,
  Glory to the Lamb,
  Glory to the Lamb.

2 My sins are washed away by the blood of the Lamb,
  Glory to the Lamb, etc.

3 I've washed my garments white in the blood of the Lamb.

4 I've lost the fear of death, thro' the blood of the Lamb.

5 The martyrs overcame by the blood of the Lamb.

6 I soon shall gain the skies thro' the blood of the Lamb.

## 86

I am saved! I am saved!
  Jesus bids me go free;
He has bought with a price
  Even me, even me.

Cho—Hallelujah, Hallelujah,
  Hallelujah to my Saviour;
  Hallelujah, Hallelujah,
  Hallelujah, Amen.

2 I am cleansed! I am cleansed!
   I am "whiter than snow;"
  He is mighty to save,
   This I know, this I know.

3 Wondrous love! wondrous love!
   Now the gift I receive;
  I have rest in his word,
   I believe, I believe.

4 I was weak—I am strong
   In the power of his might;
  And my darkness he turns,
   Into light, into light.

No. 87.
# WILL IT PAY?

N. C. N.  Music by GEO. L. BROWN.

2 Will it pay, in the conflict with sin,
 Thus to barter this soul's life away?
 Though the pleasures of time you may win,
 After all do you think it will pay?—CHO.

3 If a comrade invite you to drink,
 Or engage for some wager to play,
 I beseech you, my friend, stop and think,
 Consider the cost, will it pay?—CHO.

4 Will it pay to lose heaven for a cup
 That will only bring grief and dismay?
 Oh, then why will ye die, give it up!
 Oh, break off from its charms while you may!—CHO.

## No. 88.
# LET ME DIE.

Arr. by G. L. BROWN.

1. { O God! my heart doth long for thee, Let me die! Let me die!
   { Now set my soul at lib-er-ty; Let me die! Let me die!
D.C. My Sav-iour calls me—I'm going forth, Let me die! Let me die!

Die to the trif-ling things of earth, They're now to me of lit-tle worth;

2 Thy slaying power in me display;
  Let me die!
  I must be dead from day to day;
  Let me die!
  Dead to the world and its applause,
  To all its customs, fashions, laws,
  Of those who hate the trembling cross.
  Let me die!

3 My friends may say I'll ruined be
  If I die!
  If I leave all and follow thee,
  But I'll die!
  Their arguments will never weigh
  Nor stand the trying Judgment day;
  Help me to cast them all away.
  Let me die!

4 Oh, I must die to scoffs and sneers;
  Let me die!
  I must be freed from slavish fears;
  Let me die!
  So dead that no desire shall rise
  To appear good, or great, or wise,
  In any but my Saviour's eyes.
  Let me die!

5 If Christ would live and reign in me
  I must die!
  Like him I crucified must be;
  I must die!

Lord, drive the nails, nor heed the groans,
My flesh may writhe and make its moans,
But this the way and this alone
  I must die!

6 Begin at once to drive the nail;
  Let me die!
  O suffer not my heart to fail;
  Let me die!
  Jesus, I look to thee for power,
  T' enable me t' endure the hour
  When crucified by Sovereign power
  I shall die!

7 When I am dead, then, Lord, to thee
  I will live!
  My time, my strength, my all to thee
  Will I give!
  Oh, may the Son now make me free;
  Here, Lord, I give my all to thee
  For time and all eternity,
  I will live!

8 The carnal mind once bothered me
  But it died!
  He sanctified and made me free
  So it died!
  So dead that no desire shall rise
  To appear good, or great, or wise,
  In any but my Saviour's eyes.
  So I live.

# HIGHWAY HYMNAL. 51

## 89

All for Jesus, all for Jesus,
All my being's ransomed powers,
All my thoughts and words and doings,
All my days and all my hours.

Cho—All for Jesus gladly I resign,
All for Jesus, He alone is mine,
Blessed Jesus, all for thee,
Thou art all in all to me.

2 Let my hands perform his bidding,
Let my feet run in his ways,
Let my eyes see Jesus only,
Let my lips speak forth his praise.

3 Worldlings prize their gems of beauty,
Cling to gilded toys of dust,
Boast of wealth and fame and pleasure,
Only Jesus will I trust.

4 Since my eyes were fixed on Jesus,
I've lost sight of all beside,
So enchained my spirit's vision,
Looking at the Crucified.

5 O what wonder! how amazing!
Jesus, glorious King of Kings,
Deigns to call me His beloved,
Lets me rest beneath his wings.

## 90

Original from "The Highway."

He has washed away my sin,
Glory to the name of Jesus,
He has made me whole again,
Glory to the name of Jesus.

Cho—O, precious is the flow,
That makes me white as snow;
No other fount I know,
Glory to the name of Jesus.

2 Now he cleanseth even me,
Now his blood is all my plea.

3 He does now for sin atone,
And he claims me for his own.

4 Through the blood I've rest and peace,
This is all my righteousness.

5 He now sanctifies my soul,
Cleanses me and keeps me whole.

6 Since he washed each stain away,
This my song from day to day.

7 He my King, now reigns in me,
While I serve him I am free.
[H. V. Ardrey.

## 91

Fade, fade each earthly joy, Jesus is mine!
Break every tender tie, Jesus is mine!
Dark is the wilderness, Earth has no resting-place;
Jesus alone can bless, Jesus is mine!

2 Tempt not my soul away, Jesus is mine!
Here would I ever stay, Jesus is mine!
Perishing things of clay, Born but for one brief day,
Pass from my heart away! Jesus is mine!

3 Farewell, ye dreams of night, Jesus is mine!
Lost in this dawning light, Jesus is mine!
All that my soul has tried, Left but a dismal void,
Jesus has satisfied, Jesus is mine!

4 Farewell mortality, Jesus is mine!
Welcome eternity, Jesus is mine!
Welcome, O, loved and blest, welcome sweet scenes of rest,
Welcome my Saviour's breast, Jesus is mine!

## 92

I am coming to the cross,
I am poor and weak and blind;
I am counting all but dross,
I shall full salvation find.

Cho—I am trusting Lord, in thee;
Bless'd Lamb of Calvary;
Humbly at thy cross I bow;
Jesus saves me—saves me now.

2 Long my heart has sighed for thee,
Long has evil dwelt within;
Jesus sweetly speaks to me;
"I will cleanse you from all sin."

3 Here I give up all to thee,
Friends, and time, and earthly store;
oul and body thine to be—
Wholly thine for evermore.

4 In the promises I trust,
In the cleansing blood confide.
I am prostrate in the dust,
I with Christ am crucified.

5 Jesus comes, he fills my soul,
Perfected in him I am,
I am every whit made whole,
Glory, glory to the Lamb.—
Wm. McDonald.

## 93

Rev. L. Hartsough, with per.

I hear thy welcome voice
That calls me Lord, to Thee.
For cleansing in thy precious blood
That flowed on Calvary.

Cho—I am coming Lord!
Coming now to Thee!
Wash me, cleanse me, in the blood
That flowed on Calvary.

2 Tho' coming weak and vile,
Thou dost my strength assure;
Thou dost my vileness fully cleanse,
Till spotless all and pure.

3 'Tis Jesus calls me on
To perfect faith and love,
To perfect hope, and peace, and trust,
For earth and heaven above.

4 'Tis Jesus who confirms,
The blessed work within,
By adding grace to welcomed grace,
Where reigned the power of sin.

5 And he the witness gives
To loyal hearts and free,
That every promise is fulfilled,
If faith but brings the plea.

6 All hail, the atoning blood!
All hail, redeeming grace!
All hail, the gift of Christ, our Lord,
Our Strength and Righteousness!

## No. 94
## PERFECT LOVE FOUND.

Arr.          Music by GEO. L. BROWN.

1. O glorious theme of perfect love! It
lifts my soul to things above;
It bears on eagles' wings;
It gives my ravish'd soul a taste,
And makes for me a constant feast,
With Jesus' priests and kings.

2.
Rejoicing now in earnest hope,
I stand, and from the mountain top
  See all the land below;
Rivers of milk and honey rise,
And all the fruits of paradise
  In endless plenty grow.

3.
A land of corn, and wine, and oil,
Favor'd with God's peculiar smile,
  With every blessing blest;
There dwells the Lord our Righteousness,
And keeps his own in perfect peace,
  And everlasting rest.

4.
I said, let me at once go up;
No more on this side Jordan stop,
  But now the land possess;
This moment end my legal years;
Sorrows and sins, and doubts and fears,
  A howling wilderness.

5.
'Twas then my Joshua brought me in!
Cast out my foes; the inbred sin,
  The carnal mind removed;
His purchase there did he divide;
And O! with all the sanctified
  Gave me a lot of love.

## No. 95.
# O FOUNT OF CLEANSING.

Music by GEO. L. BROWN.

1. Beneath the glorious throne above, The crystal fountain springing,
A river full of life and love Is joy and gladness bringing.

2. Thro' all my soul its waters flow, Thro' all my senses stealing;
And deep within my heart I know The consciousness of healing.

CHORUS.
Oh, fount of cleasing, flowing free, That fount is opened wide to me,
Its waters wash me white as snow; Glory to God!

3 The barren wastes are fruitful lands,
The desert blooms with roses,
And He, the glory of all lands,
His lovely face discloses.

4 My sun no more goes down by day,
My moon no more is waning;
My feet run swift the SHINING WAY,
The heavenly portals gaining.

5 O depth of mercy, breadth of grace,
O love of God unbounded!
My soul is lost in sweet amaze,
O wondrous love confounded!

## No. 96.
## O THOU GOD OF MY SALVATION.

Arranged by GEO. L. BROWN.

1. { O Thou God of my sal-va-tion, My Redeemer from all sin; }
   { Moved by thy di-vine compassion, Who hast died my heart to win, }

I will praise thee, I will praise thee; Where shall I thy praise be-gin?

2 Though unseen, I love the Saviour,
  He hath brought salvation near;
  Manifests his pard'ning favor;
  And when Jesus doth appear,
  Soul and body, soul and body
  Shall his glorious image bear.

3 While the angel choirs are crying—
  Glory to the great I AM,
  I with them will still be vying—
  Glory! glory to the Lamb!
  O how precious, O how precious
  Is the sound of Jesus' name!

4 Angels now are hov'ring round us
  Unperceived amid the throng:
  Wond'ring at the love that crown'd us,
  Glad to join the holy song:
  Hallelujah, hallelujah,
  Love and praise to Christ belong!

## 97
## Guide me, O Thou, etc.

1 Guide me, O Thou great Jehovah,
  Pilgrim to the heav'nly land,
  I am weak, but thou art mighty,
  Hold me with thy powerful hand;
  Bread of heaven, bread of heaven,
  Feed me till I want no more.

2 Open now the crystal fountain
  Whence the healing waters flow;
  Let the fiery, cloudy pillar
  Lead me all my journey through;
  Strong Deliverer, strong Deliverer,
  Be thou still my strength and shield.

3 When I tread the verge of Jordan
  May I still in thee confide,
  Bear me through the swelling current,
  Land me safe on Canaan's side;
  Songs of praises, songs of praises,
  I will ever give to thee.

## 98
## Dismission.

1 Lord, dismiss us with thy blessing,
  Fill our hearts with joy and peace;
  Let us, each thy love possessing,
  Triumph in redeeming grace;
  O, refresh us, O, refresh us,
  Traveling through this wilderness.

2 Thanks we give and adoration,
  For thy gospel's joyful sound;
  May the fruits of thy salvation
  In our hearts and lives abound;
  May thy presence, may thy presence
  With us evermore be found.

3 So, whene'er the signal's given
  Us from earth to call away,
  Borne on angels' wings to heaven,
  Glad the summons to obey.—
  May we, ready, may we, ready,
  Rise and reign in endless day.

## 99
## Children of Heaven.

1 Children of the heavenly King,
  As we journey let us sing;
  Sing our Saviour's worthy praise,
  Glorious in his works and ways.

2 We are traveling home to God
  In the way our fathers trod;
  They are happy now, and we
  Soon their happiness shall see.

3 Oh, ye banished seed, be glad;
  Christ our Advocate is made:
  Us to save our flesh assumes,—
  Brother to our souls becomes.

4 Fear not, brethren, joyful stand
  On the borders of our land;
  Jesus Christ, our Father's Son,
  Bids us undismayed go on.

5 Lord! obediently we'll go,
  Gladly leaving all below:
  Only thou our Leader be,
  And we still will follow thee.

## No. 100.
# LET US KNEEL AROUND THE ALTAR.

Arranged by GEO. L. BROWN.

2 Nay, but I yield, I yield;
　I can hold out no more,
　I sink by dying love compell'd,
　And own thee conqueror.

3 Though late I all forsake;
　My friends, my all, resign;
　Gracious Redeemer, take, O take
　And seal me ever thine.

4 Come and possess me whole,
　Nor hence again remove;
　Settle and fix my wav'ring soul
　With all thy weight of love.

*Second Chorus.*
Jesus paid it all,
　All to him I owe,
In that fountain filled with blood
He washes white as snow.

## 101

The blood of Christ now cleanses me,
Now cleanses me, now cleanses me,
The blood of Christ now cleanses me.

Cho—As soon as I believe,
    As soon as I believe,
    As soon as I believe,
    The blood of Christ now cleanses me
    As soon as I believe.

2 See all your sins on Jesus laid,
They're washed as white as snow.

3 No Jewish type could cleanse me so,
'Tis Jesus blood alone.

4 I stagger not through unbelief,
For God hath spoke the word.

5 O, come poor sinner, believe the truth,
That Jesus died for you.

6 O death to me has lost its sting
I've Jesus in my heart.

7 Soon, soon I'll soar to realms above,
And reign with Jesus there.

## 102

From "Songs of Triumph," with per.

"My grace is sufficient for thee;"
I sing the sweet words o'er and o'er;
His promise my comfort shall be,
The strength of my heart evermore.

Cho—Sufficient for me, sufficient for me,
His strength so abundant and free,
In sorrow or pain this joy shall remain,
His grace is sufficient for me.

2 Sufficient to cleanse, and to keep
My hunger and thirst all supplied,
The fountain of mercy is deep,
The streams of salvation are wide.

3 Each day has its trials and cares,
Each day has its help for my need,
Each pathway its thorns and its snares,
But I sing while His promise I read.

4 His might shall my weakness sustain,
His fulness my portion shall be,
His pow'r made perfect in pain,
His purpose made perfect in me.

## 103

From "Songs of Triumph," with per.

While we bow in Thy name,
O meet us again,
Fill our hearts with the light of Thy love,
May the Spirit of grace,
And the smiles of Thy face,
Gently fall on us now from above.

CHORUS

It is good to be here, it is good to be here,
Thy perfect love now drives away all our fear,
And light streaming down makes the pathway all clear,
It is good for us Lord, to be here.

2 Our souls long for thee;
O may we now see
A sin-cleansing blood-wave appear,
And feel as it rolls
In power o'er our souls,
It is good for us Lord, to be here.

3 Thou art with us, we know;
We feel the sweet flow
Of the sin-cleansing wave's gladd'ning tide;
We are washed from our sin,
Made all holy within,
And in Jesus we sweetly abide.

## 104

Revised. Please sing as below.

Oh, how happy are they,
Who the Saviour obey,
And have laid up their treasure above,
Tongue can never express,
That sweet comfort and peace,
Of a soul in the fulness of love.

2 That sweet comfort was mine,
When the cleansing divine,
I received through the blood of the Lamb.
What a joy I received,
When my heart first believed,
What a heaven in Jesus's name.

3 'Tis a heaven below,
My Redeemer to know,
And the angels can do nothing more,
Than to fall at His feet,
And the story repeat,
And the lover of sinners adore.

4 Jesus all the day long
Is my joy and my song,
Oh! that all His salvation might see!
He hath cleansed me, I cried;
And I'm now sanctified,
O, exalt and adore him with me.

## 105

Hear the gentle voice that calls thee,
Come and see, come and see;
Jesus at the door of mercy,
Waits for thee, waits for thee,
To a kindly shelter nigh,
Haste, O haste thee, quickly fly.

CHORUS.

O, the Saviour is standing at the door,
O, the Saviour is standing at the door.
Wilt thou let him in He will cleanse thy sin,
O, the Saviour is standing at the door.

2 Art thou weary? lay thy burden
At the cross, at the cross,
Count this world and all its pleasures,
Only dross, only dross;
Come to Jesus, wounded soul,
He alone can make thee whole,

3 Art thou hungry? he will give the e
Living bread, living bread;
Lo, a table now before thee,
Richly spread, richly spread;
When such heavenly food is thine
Wilt thou in a desert pine?

4 Art thou thirsty? cooling waters,
Pure and free, pure and free,
From the spring of life eternal,
Flows for thee, flows for thee,
Travelers drink, O, drink again,
Healing balm for every pain.

## No. 106.
## PRAISE THE LORD, O MY SOUL.

Arr. by G. L. BROWN.

1. The King's highway of holiness, Glory hallelujah;
   I'll go for all his paths are peace,............Praise ye the Lord.

CHO. Praise the Lord, O my soul! Glory hallelujah, Praise ye the Lord.

2 I've 'listed during all this war,
Content to have a soldier's fare.

3 This war is all my soul's delight,
I love the thickest of the fight.

4 The hottest of the fight has just begun,
And who will stand and never run?

5 We want no cowards in this band,
We call for full salvation men.

6 Ye fully sanctified march on,
Until the conquest ye have won.

7 We'll sing and pray and we'll believe,
And sinners shall the truth receive.

8 We'll tell to sinners all around
What a dear Savior we have found.

9 I'll tell you when I feel the best,
It's just while I am being blest.

10 I have the witness now within,
The blood now cleanseth from all sin.

11 I now do know he saves my soul,
He sanctifies and makes me whole.

12 The blessed Jesus is my friend,
And he'll go with me to the end.

13 Oh, hallelujah to the Lamb,
He makes and keeps me what I am.

## 107
## Better on Before.

1 The Lord has pardoned all my sins,
I am condemned no more.
I want to know the deeper things—
'Tis better on before.

CHO.—Better on before, better on before;
I want to know the deeper things;
'Tis better on before.

2 I praise the Lord for all he gives,
And ask for more and more;
'Twas joyous once, 'tis glorious now,
And better on before.

3 I've left the dreary wilderness,
My wanderings now are o'er,
And every day I taste new bliss;
'Tis better on before.

4 I've reached the land of perfect love,
And still I long for more;
And Jesus whispers to my soul:
'Tis better on before.

5 And when I stand on Jordan's banks,
And view the landscape o'er,
I'll cry, "Behold my Father's land,"
'Tis better on before.

6 And when I've crossed the swelling flood,
And reached the pearly door,
I'll sing anew the same old song—
'Tis better on before.

## No. 108.
## HAPPY ON THE WAY.

Arranged by G. L. BROWN.

This is the way I long have sought, Yes, bless the Lord, I'm
And mourn'd be-cause I found it not, Yes, bless the Lord, I'm
Yes, bless the Lord, I'm

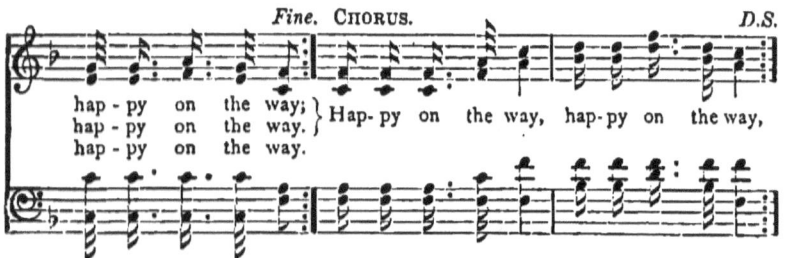

hap-py on the way;
hap-py on the way.
hap-py on the way.
Hap-py on the way, hap-py on the way,

2 The way the Holy Prophets went,
The road that leads from banishment.

3 The King's highway of holiness,
I'll go, for all his paths are peace.

4 This day my soul has caught new fire,
I feel that heaven is drawing nigher.

*Another Chorus.*
O we'll end this war down by the river,
We'll end this war down by the river's side.

## 109
## At the Fountain.

1 Of him who did salvation bring,
I'm at the fountain drinking,
I could forever think and sing,
I'm on my journey home.

CHO.—Glory to God,
I'm at the fountain drinking;
Glory to God
I'm on my journey home.

2 Ask but his grace and lo! 'tis given,
Ask and he turns your hell to heaven.

3 Tho' sin and sorrow wound my soul,
Jesus, thy balm will make me whole.

4 Let all the world fall down and know,
That none but God such love can show.

5 Where'er I am where'er I move
I meet the object of my love.

6 Insatiate to this spring I fly,
I drink, and yet am ever dry.

7 Salvation friends is ever free,
O! come, yes, come along with me.

8 Jesus, has bought us with his blood,
Come walk with me along this road.

9 The living water, O! how sweet,
Do come and drink, I oft repeat.

10 O! wondrous bliss O! joy sublime,
I've Jesus with me all the time.

11 I do believe without a doubt
That Christians have a right to shout.

12 Though wicked men revile my name,
I'll shun no cross, I fear no shame.

## No. 110.
# SAVED BY PRAYER.
*(A vision of death.)*

V. S. CASE.         Music by GEO. L. BROWN.

1. { I have stood on the banks of Jordan, I have
      My feet were bathed in its i-cy waves,..............
   trod-den the riv-er's brink;
   .......... .................. And I al-most stooped to drink.
   I came so near I could almost hear The songs the an-gels sing;
   And in the hush I felt the brush Of an un-seen an-gel's wing.

2 And one came back from the grave's
    embrace—
Ev'n one who had long been dead—
With her filmy eyes and her ashen face,
And stood beside my bed,
And whispered low: "'Tis your time
    to go;
I'll show you the way to tread."
And I could see she was beck'ning me
To follow where she led.

3 I looked again, and 'tween us twain
Yawned a chasm, deep and wide;
I saw her stand with outstretched hand
Upon the other side.
And I saw a harp of wondrous mold
Across this deep, dark way,
But I could not reach those chords of
    gold,
And I knew not how to play.

## SAVED BY PRAYER. Concluded.

4 "O! who would teach me if I could reach
  Those chords?" I sadly thought;
  When all golden bright, illumed with light,
  A shining book was brought,
  And opened wide by my angel guide,
  And placed across the strands
  Before my face, and held in place
  By unseen angels' hands.

5 And then I thought, "Oh, I could reach
  Those songs, I know I could;"
  And I stretched my hands, but could not reach
  To where the vision stood.
  And I heard a voice bid me rejoice,
  For I soon might learn to sing;
  But I could not know those songs below—
  They were anthems of the king.

6 And even now my cheek and brow
  Were damp with the dews of death;
  And my heart stood still with an awful chill,
  And I struggled hard for breath.
  And the watchers knew by the ashen hue
  That settled on my face,
  And the struggling breath, that the hour of death
  Was coming with rapid pace.

7 And they thought he'd come to our lonely room
  Long ere the dawn of day:
  When hand in hand a little band
  Knelt by my couch to pray.
  Oh, wondrous power! that every hour
  I felt a swift release
  From every pain, and once again
  I felt the hand of peace.

8 And the ashen hue left cheek and brow,
  And I ceased to gasp for breath;
  And I fell asleep in a slumber deep,
  But not the sleep of death.
  And I surely felt, as they lowly knelt,
  God's power was there to save;
  And I know 'twas he that has given me
  My life from the brink of the grave.

## No 111
## FROM EVERY STORMY WIND THAT BLOWS.
Arranged by GEO. L. BROWN.

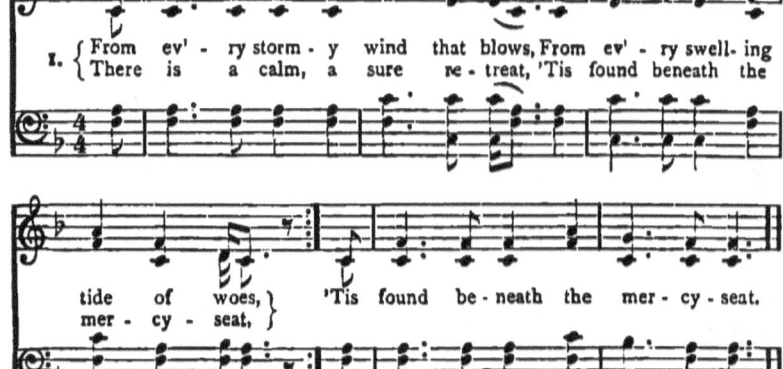

1. From ev'ry storm-y wind that blows, From ev'ry swell-ing
   There is a calm, a sure re-treat, 'Tis found beneath the
   tide of woes,
   mer-cy-seat,
   'Tis found be-neath the mer-cy-seat.

2 There is a place where Jesus sheds
  The oil of gladness on our heads;
  A place than all besides more sweet—
  It is the blood-bought mercy-seat.

3 There is a scene where spirits blend,
  Where friend holds fellowship with friend;
  Tho' sunder'd far, by faith they meet
  Around one common mercy-seat.

4 Ah! whither could we flee for aid
  When tempted, desolate, dismay'd?
  Or how the hosts of hell defeat
  Had suff'ring saints no mercy-seat?

5 There, there, on eagles' wings we soar,
  And sin and sense molest no more;
  And heaven comes down our souls to greet,
  While glory crowns the mercy-seat.

4. If he says you soon will sin,
   Still keep trusting in the Lord;
   Tell him: "not till I begin,
   For I'm trusting in the Lord."

5. God has promised thus to keep
   While you're trusting in the Lord;
   And His angels never sleep,
   So keep trusting in the Lord.

## 113

Reprint from "The Highway."

Mercy's gate stands open wide,
Enter by the blood of Jesus;
Since my Lord was crucified,
Enter by the blood of Jesus.

Cho—Oh, glory, I have found,
True blessings do abound,
Only on promised ground;
Enter by the blood of Jesus.

2 Enter now the "holy place,"
Christ unveils his shining face.

3 Here is pardon, full and free,
Cleansing, too, by faith I see.

4 You by faith may now prevail;
Pass beyond the "second veil."

## 114

Mrs. M. J. Everett. All rights given to "The Highway."

I saw a happy pilgrim,
In shining garments clad,
Traveling up the mountain,
It seemed that he was glad;
His back did bear no burden,
He'd laid it at the cross:
The blood of Christ his Saviour
Had cleansed him from all dross.

Cho—‖Soon palms of victory, crowns of glory,
Palms of victory I shall wear.‖

2 The summer sun was shining,
But he had found a shield—
A covert in the desert—
Upon life's battle-field;
His soul was filled with glory,
As he kept pressing on;
He heard no other music,
But what was heaven-born.

3 No pleasure in sin's arbor
Could catch his eye or ear;
The precious name of Jesus
Was all he loved to hear.
Thus he kept pressing onward,
Delighted with the way,
And shouting "Glory! glory!"
To Jesus all the day.

4 I saw him in the morning,
On Canaan's sunny plain,
Gathering for his Master
The rich and golden grain;
He bound it up in bundles,
Until the angels came,
To gather in the harvest,
In heaven his happy home.

5 I saw him in midsummer,
Still happy on his way;
He'd reached the land of Beulah,
Where birds sing night and day;
He found a store of honey,
And wine upon the lees,
And fruit in rich abundance
Upon life's living trees.

6 I saw him in the evening,
Life's sun was bending low,
He'd reached the golden city,
His robes still white as snow;
He joined the bridal cortege,
And drank of the new wine,
And now among the angels,
Eternally doth shine.

## 115

From the Holiness Press.

I saw a blood-washed traveler,
In garments white as snow,
While traveling on the highway,
Where heavenly breezes blow.
His path was full of trial,
And yet his face was bright,
And he shouted as he journeyed,
"I'm glad the burden's light."

Cho—‖"Soon palms of victory, crowns of glory,
Palms of victory I shall wear."‖

2 I saw him in the conflict,
Where all around was strife,
Where wicked men and devils
Conspired to take his life;
I saw him cast in prison,
A dungeon dark as night,
And still I heard him shouting,
"I'm glad the burden's light."

3 I saw him led from prison,
And chained unto the stake;
And heard him shout triumphant,
"'Tis all for Jesus sake!"
He saw the fire kindled,
The fagots blazing high,
And said, "The yoke is easy—
The burden is so light."

4 I saw the flames surround him;
His body racked with pain;
But he shouted, "Jesus saves me;—
I know that death is gain!"
Then casting his eyes upward
Before he took his flight,
I heard him faintly whisper,
"I'm glad the burden's light."

5 I saw his soul departing,
It seemed the veil was rent,
And I could see the angels
That Christ, the Lord, had sent,
They bore him to the Saviour,
The ever-blessed Son,
A saint made meet for glory,
And Jesus said, "Well Done."

## 116

What a friend we have in Jesus,
All our sins and griefs to bear;
What a privilege to carry,
Everything to God in prayer.
O, what peace we often forfeit,
O, what needless pain we bear,
All because we do not carry,
Everything to God in prayer.

2 Have we trials and temptations?
Is there trouble anywhere?
We should never be discouraged,
Take it to the Lord in prayer.
Can we find a friend so faithful,
Who will all our sorrows share?
Jesus knows our every weakness,
Take it to the Lord in prayer.

3 Are we weak and heavy laden,
Cumbered with a load of care?
Precious Saviour, still our refuge,
Take it to the Lord in prayer.
Do thy friends despise, forsake thee?
Take it to the Lord in prayer;
In His arms He'll take and shield thee,
Thou wilt find a solace there.

Rev. H. Bonar.

## No. 117.
## DRAW ME NEARER.

G. L. B.  Arr. by GEO. L. BROWN.

2.

Draw me nearer, Jesus, nearer,
Other refuge have I none;
When the sky o'erspreads with terror,
Leave, oh, leave me not alone.
I am trusting, I am trusting,
All my soul is stayed on Thee;
Draw me nearer, Jesus, nearer,
Let me now Thy glory see.

3.

Draw me nearer, Jesus, nearer,
Make, oh, make me pure within;
Let my way shine brighter, clearer,
Cleanse and keep me free from sin.
Leave me never, leave me never,
Holy One, with me abide,
Seal me Thine, all Thine forever,
'Till I sweep beyond the tide.

# THE GOSPEL LIFE-BOAT.

Music by GEO. L. BROWN.

## No. 121
## THE WHITE PILGRIM.

Arranged by GEO. L. BROWN.

1. I came to the spot where the white pil-grim lay, And

pen-sive-ly stood by the tomb, When in a low whis-per I heard something say: "How sweet-ly I sleep here a-lone."

2 "The tempest may howl, and the wild thunders roll,
And the gathering storms may arise,
Yet calm are my feelings, at peace is my soul,
And the tears are all wiped from my eyes,"

3 "Go tell all the friends that to me were so dear,
To weep not for one that is gone,
For the hand that once led me through scenes dark and drear,
Has sweetly conducted me home.

4 "The cause of my Master compell'd me from home,
I bade my companion farewell;
I left my sweet children, who now for me mourn,
In far distant regions to dwell.

5 "I wander'd, an exile and stranger below,
To publish salvation abroad,
The trump of the gospel endeavour'd to blow,
Inviting poor sinners to God.

6 "But when, among strangers and far from my home,
No kindred or relative nigh,
I met the contagion and sank in the tomb,
My spirit ascended on high."

### HIS WIDOW.

7 I call'd at the house of the mourner below,
I enter'd the mansion of grief;
The tears of deep sorrow most freely did flow—
I tried, but could give no relief.

8 There sat a lone widow dejected and sad,
By affliction and sorrow oppress'd;
And here were her children in mourning array'd,
And sighs were escaping each breast.

9 I spoke to the widow concerning her grief,
I ask'd her the cause of her woe;
And why there was nothing to give her relief,
Or soothe her deep sorrow below.

10 She look'd at her children, then look'd upon me;
That look I can never forget;
More eloquent far than a seraph can be,
It spoke of the trials she met.

11 "The hand of affliction falls heavily now;
I am left with my children to mourn;
The friend of my youth is silent and low,
In yonder cold grave-yard alone!

12 "But why should I mourn, or feel to complain,
Or think that fortune is hard?
Have I met with affliction—'tis truly his gain—
He's enter'd the joy of his Lord!

13 "His work is completed and finish'd below;
His last tear is fallen, I trust;
He has preach'd his last sermon and met his last foe;
Has conquer'd, and now is at rest!"

## 122

From "Songs of Triumph." With per.

At the sounding of the trumpet, when the saints are gather'd home,
We will greet each other by the crystal sea,
With the friends and all the lov'd ones there awaiting us to come,
What a gath'ring of the faithful that will be.

CHO—What a gath'ring, gath'ring,
At the sounding of the glorious jubilee!
What a gath'ring, gath'ring,
What a gath'ring of the faithful that will be.

2 When the angel of the Lord proclaims that time shall be no more,
We will gather and the saved and ransom'd see,
Then to meet again together on the bright celestial shore,
What a gath'ring of the faithful that will be.

3 At the great and final judgment, when the hidden come to light,
When the Lord in all his glory we shall see,
At the bidding of our Saviour, "Come ye blessed to my right,"
What a gath'ring of the faithful that will be.

4 When the golden harps are sounding, and the angel bands proclaim,
In triumphant strains the glorious jubilee,
Then to meet and join to sing the song of Moses and the Lamb,
What a gath'ring of the faithful that will be.

## 123

From the "Revivalist."

Down at the cross where my Saviour died,
Down where for cleansing from sin I cried,
There to my heart was the blood applied,
    Glory to His name.

Cho—Glory to his name,
    Glory to his name,
    There to my heart was the blood applied,
    Glory to his name.

2 I am so wondrously saved from sin,
Jesus so sweetly abides within,
Here at the cross where he took me in,
    Glory to his name.

3 O, precious fountain, that saves from sin,
I am so glad I have entered in,
Here Jesus saves me and keeps me clean,
    Glory to his name.

4 Come to the fountain so rich and sweet,
Cast thy poor soul at the Saviour's feet,
Plunge in just now and be made complete,
    Glory to his name.

## 124

"Songs of Triumph," with per.

Redeemed, how I love to proclaim it,
    Redeemed by the blood of the Lamb;
Redeemed thro' His infinite mercy,
    His child and forever I am.

Cho—Redeemed, redeemed,
    Redeemed by the blood of the Lamb;
    Redeemed, redeemed
    His child and forever I am.

2 Redeemed, and so happy in Jesus,
No language my rapture can tell,
I know that the light of his presence,
With me doth continually dwell.

3 I think of my blessed Redeemer,
I think of Him all the day long,
I sing for I cannot be silent,
His love is the theme of my song.

4 I know I shall see in his beauty,
The King in whose law I delight,
Who lovingly guardeth my footsteps,
And giveth me songs in the night.

5 I know there's a crown that is waiting
In yonder bright mansion for me,
And soon with the spirits made perfect,
At home with the Lord I shall be.

## 125

O, happy day that fixed my choice
    On Thee, my Saviour and my God!
Well may this glowing heart rejoice,
    And tell its raptures all abroad.

2 O, happy bond that seals my vows
To him who merits all my love;
Let cheerful anthems fill his house,
While to that sacred shrine I move.

3 'Tis done, the great transaction's done;
I am my Lord's and he is mine;
He drew me, and I followed on,
Charmed to confess the voice divine.

4 Now rest, my long divided heart,
Fixed on this blissful center, rest;
Nor ever from my Lord depart!
With him of every good possessed.

5 High heaven, that heard the solemn vow,
That vow renewed, shall daily hear,
Till in life's latest hour I bow,
And bless in death a bond so dear.

## 126

Goliath, the Philistine, comes
    To-day, to-day,
To meet the armies of the Lord,
    To-day, to-day.

Cho—'Tis the good old way,
    The righteous way.
    I'm bound to go to heaven
    In this holy way.

2 A helmet of brass upon his head, &c.,
And clad with weighty coat of mail, &c.

3 Say brother have you got your shield,
To meet Goliath on the field.

4 The hosts of hell are boasting much,
To drive the armies of the Lord.

5 The Lord Jehovah is our shield,
We kill Goliath just the same.

6 Say sinners will you turn to God,
Walk in the way the fathers trod.

7 There's pardon offered full and free,
And cleansing too for you and me.

8 There is a fountain filled with blood,
Then plunge beneath the cleansing flood.

9 The blood of Christ it cleanseth me,
From sin and bondage I am free.

10 The breast plate, helmet, sword and shield,
Equips the christian for the field.

## 127

Rev. L. Hartsough, with per.

Lord, in the strength of grace,
    With a glad heart and free,
Myself, my residue of days,
    I consecrate to thee.

2 Thy ransomed servant, I
Restore to thee thine own;
And from this moment live or die,
To serve my God alone.

## 128

Sad and weary with my longing,
    Fill'd with shame, because of sin;
As I am in conscious weakness,
    Here I would salvation win,

Cho—All I have I leave with Jesus,
    I am counting it but dross,
    I am coming to the Master,
    I am clinging, to the cross,
Clinging, clinging, clinging to the cross.

2 O, the joy of knowing Jesus,
It is dawning on my soul;
I am finding full salvation,
And the pow'r that makes me whole.

3 O, refine me by thy Spirit;
Make my earthly life sublime,
With my heart a home for Jesus,
Till I'm done with earth and time.

## No. 129.
## THE GOSPEL TRAIN.

GEO. W. PETTY.            GEO. L. BROWN.

1. The gos-pel train is com-ing, I see her just at hand,
 I hear her car wheels roll - ing Tri-umphant thro' the land.
2. The way is free, and all may go, The rich and poor are there,
 No sec-ond-class on board this train, No difference in the fare.
3. The tel-e-graph is by the way, It reach-es up to God,
 To tell our friends who've gone be-fore That we are on the road.

CHORUS.
Get on board, chil-dren, O chil-dren, get on board!
Get on board, chil-dren, There's room for ma-ny more!

4.
There's Moses, Noah, Abraham,
And all the prophets, too;
Our friends in Christ are on this train,
Oh, what a heav'nly crew!

5.
She's coming round the mountain,
By the river and the lake,
Our Saviour he's on board this train
Controlling steam and brake.

6.
I hear the steam and whistle,
I'm sure she'll be on time,
Poor sinner, you're forever lost
If once you're left behind.

7.
She's halting at the station,
Oh! must we say farewell,
Poor sinner, must we leave you
On the dreary road to hell?

### No. 130.
## ONE DAY NEARER HOME.

Words by PHŒBE CARY.    Music by GEO. L. BROWN.

1. One sweet - ly solemn thought Comes to me o'er and o'er; I'm near - er home to-day Than I have been before.
2. Near - er my Father's house, Where many man-sions be; Nearer the great white throne, Nearer the Jas-per sea.
3. For e - ven now my feet May stand up - on its brink; I may be near - er home, Nearer than now I think.

CHORUS.

Near-er my home, Near-er my home, Near-er my home to-day Than I have been before.

### No 131 LOOK TO JESUS.

Words by D. D. HAGGARD.    Music by GEO. L. BROWN.

1. In thy pet - ty care of life, Look to Je-sus. In thy doubtings, and thy
2. When the world around is drear, Look to Je-sus. When the soul is filled with
3. If thy faith is small and weak, Look to Je-sus. If thy soul rich blessings

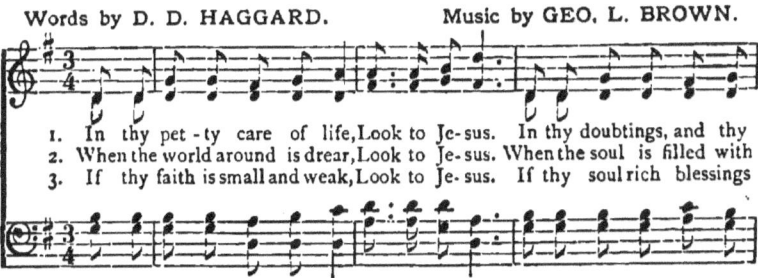

## LOOK TO JESUS. Concluded.

strife, Look to Je - sus,  In thy sor - row and thy pain,
fear, Look to Je - sus.  When the faith seems to be strong,
seek, Look to Je - sus.  If thy heart more joy would know,

Do not, do not then complain, Look to Je - sus, Look to Je - sus.
And the heart is filled with song, Look to Je - sus, Look to Je - sus.
Ev - er to thy Saviour go, Look to Je - sus, Look to Je - sus.

## No. 132. CHRISTIAN SOLDIER.

Arranged by GEO. L. BROWN.

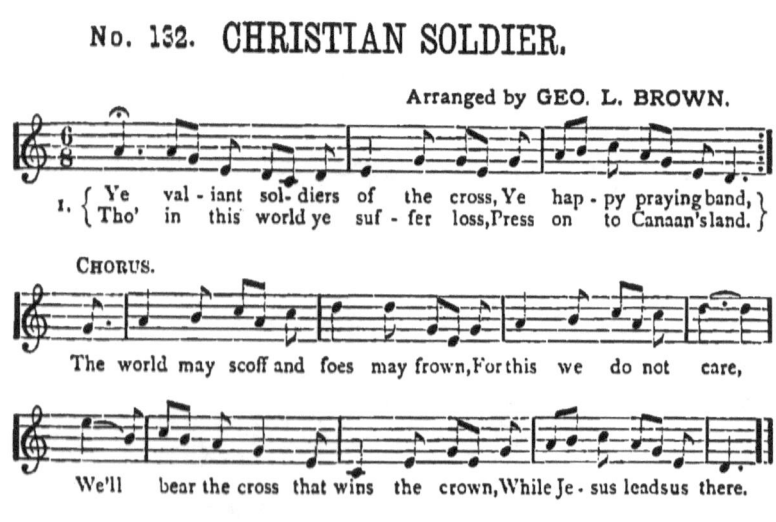

1. { Ye val - iant sol - diers of the cross, Ye hap - py praying band, }
   { Tho' in this world ye suf - fer loss, Press on to Canaan's land. }

CHORUS.

The world may scoff and foes may frown, For this we do not care,
We'll bear the cross that wins the crown, While Je - sus leads us there.

2 All earthly pleasures we forsake
   Since heaven appears in view;
   In Jesus' might we'll undertake
   To fight our passage through.

3 Oh, what a glorious shout there'll be
   When we arrive at home,
   Our friends and Jesus we shall see,
   And God shall say: "Well done!"

## 134

I've reach'd the land of corn and wine
And all its riches freely mine;
Here shines undim'd one blissful day,
For all my night has passed away.

CHORUS.

O Beulah land, sweet Beulah land,
As on thy highest mount I stand,
I look away across the sea,
Where mansions are prepared for me,
And view the shining glory shore,
My heav'n, my home for evermore!

2 The Saviour comes and walks with me,
And sweet communion here have we;
He gently leads me with his hand,
For this is heaven's border land.

3 A sweet perfume upon the breeze
Is borne from ever vernal trees,
And flow'rs that never fading grow
Where streams of life forever flow.

4 The zephyrs seem to float to me,
Sweet sounds of heav'ns melody,
As angels, with the white-robed throng,
Join in the sweet redemption song.

## 135

—Holiness Press.

I've joined the army of the Lord,
Obedient to my captain's word:
I'm now a soldier of our King,
Who always does each battle win.

CHORUS.

Oh, blessed army of the Lord,
What peace and joy it doth afford
To fight beneath the blood-stained cross,
And for his sake count all else loss,
Until the glorious war is o'er,
Then reign with Jesus evermore.

2 My Captain is the King of King's,
And 'mid the conflict often rings,
His voice to bid me forward go,
Though fierce and mighty be the foe.

3 The battle often waxes hot,
But the Commander leaves me not;
He gives me victory day by day,
And in his army I will stay.

4 My unsaved friends, with me unite,
And in this blessed army fight,—
This royal army of the Lord,
And heaven shall be your great reward.

5 Enlist at once, the armor seize,
And fling your banner to the breeze,
Go bravely forth the foe to meet,
And trophies bring to Jesus' feet.

6 And when the final battle's fought,
And satan's kingdom brought to naught,
Oh, what a mighty shout we'll raise,
And give our Captain endless praise.

## 136

Why do these doubts and fears arise,
As this poor little all of mine
I lay a living sacrifice,
All on the altar, Christ Divine.

CHORUS.

I'm fully thine; yes, wholly thine,
All on the altar Christ divine;
The word of Jesus I believe,
The Sanctifier I receive.
All on the altar I abide,
And Jesus says I'm sanctified.

2 Ah! not a moment more I'll doubt,
And not a moment longer wait;
With his own blood to sanctify,
He suffered death without the gate.

3 By faith I venture on his word,
My doubts are o'er the victory won,
He said, "The altar sanctifies;"
I just believe him—and 'tis done.

4 Thro' all my soul I feel his power,
As in the precious cleansing wave
I wash my garments white this hour,
And prove his utmost power to save.

## 137

My pilgrim days are almost o'er,
I'm waiting now on Beulah's shore,
Where birds sing in the balmy breeze,
'Mid vernal flowers and fruitful trees.

2 'Tis here my longing heart is filled,
Here every anxious thought is stilled,
A holy calmness fills my breast,
As in "sweet Beulah land" I rest.

3 No dark despair, no doubt, no gloom,
No shadows of the awful tomb!
No days of darkness, all are past,
Glory to God, I'm safe at last!

4 By faith I see the shining towers
And breathe the air from heaven's bowers;
I hear the notes that angels sing,
Wafted across, on silv'ry wing.

5 The "city gates" appear in sight,
And God himself dispels the night;
I see a white-robed company
Awaiting there to welcome me.

6 "O sing! ye ransomed of the Lord,"
He has redeemed, he has restored,
I'm waiting in "sweet Beulah's land,"
And soon shall join the shining band.
[Anon.

## 138

My all to Christ I've given,
My talents, time, and voice,
Myself, my reputation,
The lone way is my choice.

CHO—And the cross for Christ I'll cherish,
Its crucifixion bear;
All hail reproach or sorrow,
If Jesus leads me there.

## 139

I thirst thou wounded Lamb of God,
To wash me in the cleansing blood;
To dwell within thy wounds, then pain
Is sweet, and life or death is gain.

2 Take my poor heart and let it be
Forever closed to all but thee;
Seal thou my breast and let me wear
That pledge of love forever there.

## No 140
## WHAT'S THE NEWS.

1 Where'er we meet, you always say,
   What's the news? what's the news?
Pray what's the order of the day?
   What's the news? what's the news?
Oh, I have got good news to tell,
   My Saviour hath done all things well,
And triumphed over death and hell,
   That's the news! that's the news!

2 His work's reviving all around,
   That's the news! that's the news!
His saints are making sounds resound,
   That's the news! that's the news!
Poor sinners doomed in sin and woe
   Are now rejoicing as they go;
And shouting glory here below,
   That's the news! that's the news!

3 He took my sorrows all away,
   That's the news! that's the news!
He turned my darkness into day,
   That's the news! that's the news!
Yes, Jesus saves me now I know,
   His blood has washed me white as snow;
And now I'm glad His love to show,
   That's the news! that's the news!

4 And Christ, the Lord, can save you now,
   That's the news! that's the news!
Your sinful heart He can renew,
   That's the news! that's the news!
This moment if for sins you grieve,
This moment if you now believe,
A full acquittal you'll receive.
   That's the news! that's the news!

5 And now if any one should say,
   What's the news? what's the news?
Oh, tell them you are sanctified,
   That's the news! that's the news!
That you have joined the conquering band,
   And now with joy at God's command,
You're marching to the better land,
   That's the news! that's the news!

## 141
## The Promised Land.

1 I have a Father in the promised land,
   I have a Father in the promised land,
      My Father calls me, I must go
   To meet him in the promised land.

CHORUS.—I'll away, I'll away to the
      promised land,
   I'll away, I'll away to the promised land,
      My Father calls me, I must go
   To meet him in the promised land.—CHO.

2 I have a Saviour in the promised land,
   I have a Saviour in the promised land,
      My Saviour calls me, I must go
   To meet him in the promised land.—CHO.

3 I hope to meet you in the promised land,
   I hope to meet you in the promised land,
      At Jesus' feet, a joyous band,
   We'll praise him in the promised land.
        CHO.

## 142 REMEMBER ME.

*Very slow.*             Arr. by G. L. B.

CHO.—{ Re - mem - ber me, remem - ber me, O Lord, re - mem-ber me.
       { Re - mem - ber, Lord, thy dy - ing groans, And then re - mem-ber me.

1 Forever here my rest shall be,
   Close to thy bleeding side;
This all my hope, and all my plea,—
   For me the Saviour died.

2 My dying Saviour, and my God,
   Fountain for guilt and sin,
Sprinkle me ever with thy blood,
   And cleanse and keep me clean.

3 Wash me, and make me thus thine own;
   Wash me, and mine thou art;
Wash me, but not my feet alone,—
   My hands, my head, my heart.

4 Th' atonement of thy blood apply,
   Till faith to sight improve;
Till hope in full fruition die,
   And all my soul be love.

## 143

Oh, blessed fellowship divine!
Oh, joy supremely sweet!
Companionship with Jesus here,
Makes life with bliss replete.
In union with the purest one
I find my heaven on earth begun.

Cho—Oh, wondrous bliss, oh joy sublime,
I've Jesus with me all the time.
Oh wondrous bliss, oh joy sublime,
I've Jesus with me all the time.

2 I'm walking close to Jesus' side,—
So close that I can hear
The softest whisper of his love,—
In fellowship so dear,
And feel his great Almighty hand
Protects me in this hostile land.

3 I'm leaning on his loving breast,
Along life's weary way;
My path, illumined by his smiles,
Grows brighter day by day.
No foes, no woes my heart can fear,
With my Almighty Friend so near.

4 I know his shelt'ring wings of love
Are always o'er me spread,
And tho' the storms may fiercely rage,
All calm and free from dread,
My peaceful spirit ever sings
"I'll trust the covert of thy wings."
—Mary D. James.

## 144

Dear Jesus, I long to be perfectly whole;
I want thee forever to live in my soul;
Break down every idol, cast out every foe;
Now wash me, and I shall be whiter than snow.

Chorus.

Whiter than snow, yes, whiter than snow;
Now wash me and I shall be whiter than snow.

2 Dear Jesus, thou seest I patiently wait,
Come now and within me a clean heart create,
To those who have sought Thee thou never saidst No;
Now wash me and I shall be whiter than snow

3 Dear Jesus, let nothing unholy remain;
Apply thine own blood and extract every stain;
To have this blest cleansing I all things forego;
Now wash me and I shall be whiter than snow.

4 Dear Jesus, for this I most humbly entreat,
I wait, blessed Lord, at thy crucified feet;
By faith for my cleansing I see thy blood flow,
Now wash me and I shall be whiter than snow.

5 The blessing by faith I receive from above,
O, glory! my soul is made perfect in love;
My prayer has prevailed, and this moment I know
The blood is applied—I am whiter than snow.
—W. Nicholson.

## 145

Blessed Jesus, thou art mine,
All I have is wholly thine;
Thou dost dwell within my heart,
Thou dost reign in every part.

Cho—!Blessed Jesus keep me white
Keep me walking in the light.!

2 I am safe within the fold,
All my cares on thee are rolled,
I enjoy the sweetest rest,
For I'm leaning on thy breast.

3 Precious Jesus, day by day
Keep me in the holy way;
Keep my mind in perfect peace;
Every day my faith increase.

4 'Tis the happiest place to be
In the heavenlies with thee,
I have found the highest seat
For I'm sitting at thy feet.

5 Humbly at thy feet I bow,
Put thy yoke upon me now,
Keep me trusting on thine arm
Free from sin and safe from harm.

## 146

A better day is coming, a morning promised long
When girded right, with holy might, will overthrow the wrong;
When God the Lord will listen to every plaintive sigh,
And stretch his hand o'er every land, with justice by and by.

Chorus.

Coming by and by, coming by and by,
The better day is coming, the morning draweth nigh;
Coming by and by, coming by and by,
The welcome dawn will hasten on, 'tis coming by and by.

2 The boast of haughty error no more shall fill the air,
But age and youth will love the truth and spread it everywhere;
No more from want and sorrow shall come the hopeless cry,
But strife will cease, and perfect peace, will flourish by and by.

3 The tidal wave is coming, salvation full and free,
With shout and song it sweeps along, like billows of the sea;
The jubilee of holiness shall ring through earth and sky,
The dawn of grace draws on apace, tis coming by and by.

4 We're waiting, Lord, and longing, till thou shalt come again
To claim thine own, and on thy throne in peace and love to reign;
We'll wait that glorious coming till from the open sky
Our Lord shall come to take us home, He's coming by and by.

5 Oh, for that holy dawning we watch and wait and pray,
Till o'er the height the morning light shall drive the gloom away;
And when the heavenly glory shall flood the earth and sky,
We'll bless the Lord for all His word and praise Him by and by.

—Enlarged by J. P. Brooks.

No. 147.

## REID. (Double.)

C. WESLEY.  GEO. L. BROWN.

1. Oh, for a thousand tongues to sing My great Redeemer's praise;
The glories of my God and King, The triumphs of His grace.
My gracious Master and my God, Assist me to proclaim—
To spread, thro' all the earth abroad, The honors of Thy Name.

2. Jesus! the Name that charms our fears, That bids our sorrows cease;
'Tis music in the sinner's ears, 'Tis life, and health, and peace.
He breaks the pow'r of cancel'd sin, He sets the pris'ner free;
His blood can make the foulest clean; His blood availed for me.

3. He speaks; and list'ning to his voice, New life the dead receive;
The mournful, broken hearts rejoice; The humble, poor believe.
Hear Him, ye deaf; His praise, ye dumb, Your loosened tongue employ;
Ye blind, behold your Saviour come; And leap, ye lame, for joy.

## No. 149. SING ON, PRAY ON.
Arr. by GEO. L. BROWN.

1. { My Bible leads to glory, My Bible leads to glory,
   { My Bible leads to glory, .......... Ye followers of the Lamb.
   { Sing on, pray on, Ye followers of Immanuel;
   { Sing on, pray on, .......... Ye followers of the Lamb.

2 Religion makes me happy.
3 King Jesus is my Captain.
4 I long to see my Saviour.
5 Then farewell sin and sorrow.
6 We must be pure and holy.
7 The pure in heart shall see Him.
8 He gives me grace and glory.
9 He sanctifies me wholly.
10 He sweetly saves and keeps me.

## 150 EXPOSTULATION. 11s.

1. Oh, turn ye, oh, turn ye, for why will ye die, { When God in great mercy is coming so nigh?
   { Since Jesus invites you, the Spirit says, come! } And angels are waiting to welcome you home.

2 How vain the delusion, that while you delay,
  Your hearts may grow better by staying away;
  Come wretched, come starving, come just as you be,
  While streams of salvation are flowing so free.

3 And now Christ is ready your souls to receive,
  Oh, how can you question, if you will believe?
  If sin is your burden, why will you not come?
  'Tis you he bids welcome; he bids you come home

4 In riches, in pleasures, what can you obtain
  To soothe your affliction, or banish your pain,
  To bear up your spirit when summoned to die,
  Or waft you to mansions of glory on high?

5 Why will you be starving, and feeding on air?
  There's mercy in Jesus, enough and to spare;
  If still you are doubting, make trial and see,
  And prove that his mercy is boundless and free.

6 Come, give us your hand, and the Saviour your heart,
  And, trusting in heaven, we never shall part;
  Oh, how can we leave you? why will you not come?
  We'll journey together, and soon be at home.

## 151

My life flows on in endless song,
  Above earth's lamentation,
I catch the sweet, seraphic song,
  That hails a new creation?
Through all the tumult and the strife,
  I hear the music ringing,
It finds an echo in my soul—
  How can I keep from singing.

2 What though my joys and comfort die?
  The Lord, my Saviour, liveth;
What though the darkness gather round?
  Songs in the night He giveth.
No storm can shake my inmost calm,
  While to that refuge clinging;
Since Christ is Lord of heaven and earth,
  How can I keep from singing?

3 I lift my eyes; the cloud grows thin;
  I see the blue above it;
And day by day this pathway smooths,
  Since first I learned to love it.
The peace of Christ makes fresh my heart,
  A fountain ever springing;
All things are mine since I am His—
  How can I keep from singing?
                 [Miss A. Warner.

## 152

Blest be the tie that binds
  Our hearts in christian love;
The fellowship of kindred minds
  Is like to that above.

2 Before our Father's throne,
  We pour our ardent prayers,
Our fears, our aims, our hopes are one—
  Our comforts and our cares.

3 We share our mutual woes,
  Our mutual burdens bear,
And often for each other flows
  The sympathetic tear.

4 When we asunder part,
  It gives us inward pain,
But we shall still be joined in heart,
  And hope to meet again.

## 153

No. 40 "Spiritual Songs."

I have found repose for my weary soul,
  Trusting in the promise of the Savior;
And a harbor safe when the billows roll,
  Trusting in the promise of the Savior,
I will fear no foe in the deadly strife
  Trusting in the promise of the Savior,
I will bear my lot in the toil of life,
  Trusting in the promise of my Savior.

CHO—Resting on his mighty arm for ever,
  Never from his loving heart to sever,
    I will rest by grace,
    In his strong embrace,
  Trusting in the promise of the Savior.

2 I will sing my song as the days go by,
And rejoice in hope, while I live or die,
I can smile at grief, and abide in pain,
And the loss of all shall be highest gain.

3 Oh the peace and joy of the life I live,
Oh, the strength and grace only God can give,
Whosoever will my be saved to-day,
And begin to walk in the holy way.

## 154

From the "Revivalist.

Who, who are these beside the chilly wave,
Just on the borders of the silent grave,
Shouting Jesus' power to save,
"Washed in the blood of the Lamb."

CHORUS.:

"Sweeping thro' the gates," to the New Jerusalem,
"Washed in the blood of the Lamb."

2 These, these are they, who in their youthful days,
Found Jesus early, and in wisdom's ways!
Proved the fulness of his grace,
"Washed in the blood of the Lamb."

3 These, these are they, who in affliction's woes,
Ever have found in Jesus calm repose;
Such as from a pure heart flows,
"Washed in the blood of the Lamb"

4 These, these are they who in the conflict dire,
Boldly have stood amidst the hottest fire;
Jesus now says: "Come up higher,"
"Washed in the blood of the Lamb."

5 Safe, safe upon the ever-shining shore.
Sin, pain and death, and sorrow all are o'er;
Happy now and evermore,
"Washed in the blood of the Lamb."

## 155

From "Spiritual Songs."

Precious Saviour thou hast saved me,
  Thine and only thine I am.
O, the cleansing blood has reached me,
  Glory, glory to the Lamb.

CHORUS.

Glory, glory, Jesus saves me,
  Glory, glory to the Lamb;
O, the cleansing blood has reached me,
  Glory, glory to the Lamb.

2 Long my yearning heart was trying,
  To enjoy this perfect rest,—
When I gave all trying over,
  Simply trusting I was blest.

3 Trusting, trusting every moment,
  Feeling now the blood applied,
Lying in the cleansing fountain,
  Dwelling in my Saviour's side.

4 Consecrated to thy service,
  I will live and die for thee,
I will witness to thy glory,
  Of salvation full and free.

5 Yes, I will stand up for Jesus,
  He has sweetly saved my soul,
Saved me from imbred corruption
  Sanctified and made me whole.

6 Glory to the blood that bought me,
  Glory to its cleansing power,
Glory to the blood that keeps me,
  Glory, glory, evermore.

## 157

Rev. L. Hartsough, with per.

O, who'll stand up for Jesus,
The lowly Nazarene?
And raise the blood-stain'd banner
Amid the hosts of sin?

Cho—The cross of Christ I'll cherish,
Its crucifixion bear;
All hail reproach or sorrow,
If Jesus leads me there.

2 O, who will follow Jesus,
Amid reproach and shame?
While others shrink or falter,
Who'll glory in his name?

3 Though fierce may rage the battle,
And wild the storm may blow,—
Though friends may go forever,
Who will with Jesus go?

4 My all to Christ I've given,
My talents, time, and voice,
Myself, my reputation,
The lone way is my choice.

5 O, Jesus, Jesus, Jesus,
My all-sufficient friend!
Come, fold me to thy bosom,
E'en to the journey's end.

## 158

'Tis known on earth and heaven too,
'Tis sweet to me because 'tis true;
The old, old story is e'er new;
Tell me more about Jesus.

Cho—Tell me more about Jesus,
Tell me more about Jesus:
Him would I know who loved me so;
Tell me more about Jesus.

2 Earth's fairest flow'rs will droop and die,
Dark clouds o'erspread yon azure sky,
Life's dearest joys flit fleetest by;
Tell me more about Jesus.

3 When overwhelmed with unbelief,
When burdened with a blinding grief;
Come kindly then to my relief;
Tell me more about Jesus.

4 And when the glory land I see,
And take the place prepared for me,
Thro' endless years my song shall be,
Tell me more about Jesus.

## 159

We may spread our couch with roses,
And sleep through the summer day,
But the soul that in sloth reposes,
Is not in the narrow way,
If we follow the chart that is given,
We will not be at a loss,
For the only way to heaven,
Is the royal way of the cross.

2 To one who is reared in splendor,
The cross is a heavy load,
And the feet that are soft and tender,
Will shrink from the thorny road,
But the chains of the soul must be riven,
And wealth must be as dross,
For the only way to heaven,
Is the royal way of the cross.

3 Some say they will walk to-morrow,
The path they refuse to-day,
And still with their lukewarm sorrow,
They shrink from the narrow way.
What heeded the chosen eleven,
How the fortunes of life might toss,
As they follow'd the Master to heaven,
By the royal way of the cross.

## 160

(Sing to the tune "Gates Ajar.")

There is a fountain deep and wide,
Which flows for every nation,
'Twas open when the Saviour died,
And there is full salvation.

Cho—O praise the Lord, I feel, I know
That Jesus washes white as snow,
As snow, I know,
He washes white as snow.

2 By faith I reached the healing stream,
That flows from Calvary's mountain,
I plunge, and O, what joy I feel;
I know I'm in the fountain.

3 I rest my long divided heart
On Christ the sure foundation,
Who does to me new life impart
And I'm a new creation.

4 I rise on wings of love and light,
Above the world's commotion,
With heart made pure and garments white,
I'm sweeping o'er life's ocean.

## 161

Oh! I have religion,
Arn't you almost ready,
And I'll tell you what the
Lord has done for my soul.

Chorus.

Oh! sweet Canaan! I'm in the land of Canaan,
Oh! sweet Canaan! I'm on my journey home.
My home is over Jordan arn't you almost ready,
Come, I'll tell you what the Lord has done for my soul.

2 I'll tell you how I got it,
Arn't you almost ready?
And I'll tell you what the
Lord has done for my soul.

Oh, sweet Canaan,
I'm in the land of Canaan, &c.

I gave my heart to Jesus, &c.
He pardoned all my sins, &c.
He sanctified me wholly, &c.
My home is over Jordon, &c.
I'm eating grapes and honey, &c.
I'm climbing Jacob's ladder, &c.
Every round I get higher, &c.
My ship is on the ocean, &c.
My father has religion, &c.
My Mother has religion, &c.
My brother has religion, &c.
My sister has religion, &c.
I hear the Master calling, &c.
Father, mother, sister, brother, &c.
This is the blood-washed army, &c.
I'm glad I'm in this army, &c.

## No. 163.
# THE TRUMP OF JUBILEE.

R. WILLIAMS.
An old and highly popular Welsh tune.

[Music: Soprano and Bass parts with lyrics:]

1. What that voice so clear-ly sounding? 'Tis the voice that calls for thee.
What those trum-pet tones re-sounding? 'Tis the trump of Ju-bi-lee,
'Tis the trump of Ju-bi-lee. Home, ye ransomed, to your mountain, In the year of Ju-bi-lee; Wash in Si-lo, Wash in Si-lo's sacred fountain, Wash in Si-lo's sa-cred fountain, Flowing down from Cal-va-ry.

2. What that standard on the mountian?
 'Tis the holy flag of peace;
What that ever-teeming fountain?
 'Tis the fount of heavenly grace.

3. What those open gates before me?
 They are Zion's gates divine;
What those domes all crown'd with glory?
 Ransomed sinner, they are thine.

4. Who has bought me these possessions?
 Jesus, with his streaming blood;
Who atones for my transgressions?
 Christ, the suffering Lamb of God.

5. Will not Satan's wiles annoy me?
 Christ is mightier far than he;
Will not death at last destroy me?
 Death in Christ is victory.

No. 164.
## JACOB'S LADDER.
Arr. by G. L. BROWN.

1. As Jacob once travelled he was weary one day, At night on a stone for a pillow he lay, He saw in a vision a ladder so high, Its foot was on earth and its top reached the sky.

CHO. Hallelujah to Jesus, who died on the tree, To raise up this ladder of mercy for me; Press upward, press upward, the prize is in view, A crown of bright glory is waiting for you.

2 This heavenly ladder is strong and well-made,
    Tho' standing for ages, it has not decayed ;
    The feeblest may venture by faith to go up,
    And angels will guard them from bottom to top.

3 Lo! upward and downward they constantly go,
    Extending a hand to the toilers below ;
    And when a new convert sets out for the skies,
    Their shouts to the top of the ladder arise.

4 Another! another! they sing in their love,
    Is seeking his home and his treasures above :
    And angels, in glory, responding cry—Come!
    And welcome each penitent sinner up home.

5 This ladder is Jesus, the glorious God-man,
    Whose blood freely streaming from calvary ran ;
    By His great atonement to heaven we rise,
    And sing in the mansions prepared in the skies.

6 Upon it our fathers have gone to their God,
    They've finished their journey and gained their abode,
    And we are ascending and soon will be there,
    Their songs and their rapture in glory to share.

## No 165
## WHILE I BOW BEFORE THEE.

G. L. B.  
GEO. L. BROWN.

2 Jesus, I am hung'ring for thy love!
  Satisfy my thirsting soul, O Lord!
Kneeling now before Thee,
  Let me to Thine image be restored!

3 Jesus, I am waiting for Thee now!
  Thou art coming—draw nigh, draw nigh!
On the Cross which bore Thee
  I am hanging helpless—hear my cry!

## 166

1. I will sing you a song of the Lord's wondrous power,
How he saves even me from all sin.
While in darkness and dread of the great Judgment hour,
How the darkness all fled within.

2. Jesus said unto me, "I am faithful and just
To forgive if you only believe."
So I laid hold by faith in the all cleansing blood
And his pardoning grace did receive.

3. I now have peace with God through our Lord Jesus Christ
Who has washed all transgressions away;
I rejoice in his love, and delight in his word,
As I walk in the light day by day.

4. Jesus called me again to be perfect in love,
And be cleansed from the body of sin;
So I walked in the light and had faith in the blood,
And the Lord made me holy within.

5. Jesus now gives me power as I walk day by day,
In the clear light that shines on the road;
And I now take delight as I rapidly run,
In the bright shining way up to God.

6. Won't you come, sinner, come; give your heart to the Lord
And join in this glorious war;
And we'll all gain a crown in the bright world above,
When our labors and toils are all o'er.

7. You that have peace with God, come and plunge in the fount,
And be cleansed from the body of sin;
And unite in the battle with Jesus our Lord,
Have your soul full of glory within.

8. If we're true to the Lord we will soon reach our home
With the blood washed and angels above;
There with Jesus our King who redeemed us from sin,
We will show forth his glory and love.
—Wm. H. Homes.

## 167

"Gems Gospel Song," with per.

1. I am dwelling on the mountain
Where the golden sunlight gleams
O'er a land whose wondrous beauty,
Far exceeds my fondest dreams,
Where the air is pure, ethereal,
Laden with the breath of flowers
That are blooming by the fountain,
'Neath the amaranthine bowers.

Cho—O yes, this is the land of Beulah,
Blessed, blessed land of light,
Where the flowers bloom forever,
And the sun is always bright.

2. I can see far down the mountain,
Where I wandered weary years,
Often hindered in my journey,
By the ghosts of doubts and fears,
Broken vows and disappointments
Thickly sprinkled all the way;
But the spirit led unerring,
To the land I hold to-day.

3. I am drinking at the fountain,
Where I ever would abide;
For I've tasted life's pure river,
And my soul is satisfied;
There's no thirsting for life's pleasures,
Nor adorning rich and gay;
For I've found a richer treasure,
One that fadeth not away.

4. Tell me not of heavy crosses,
Nor of burdens hard to bear;
For I find this great salvation,
Makes each burden light appear;
And I love to follow Jesus,
Gladly counting all but dross,
Worldly honors all forsaking,
For the glory of the Cross.

5. O! the Cross has wondrous glory,
Oft I've proved this to be true;
When I'm in the way so narrow,
I can see a pathway through;
And how sweetly Jesus whispers,
"Take the cross, thou need'st not fear,
I have trod this way before thee,"
And the glory lingers near.

## 168

From Songs of Triumph.

Take the world but give me Jesus,
All its joys are but a name;
But his love abideth ever,
Through eternal years the same,

Cho—O the height and depth of mercy,
O the length and breadth of love.
O the fulness of redemption,
Pledge of endless life above.

2. Take the world, but give me Jesus,
Sweetest comfort of my soul;
With my Saviour watching o'er me
I can sing though billows roll.

3. Take the world, but give me Jesus,
Let me view his constant smile;
Then throughout my pilgrim journey
Light will cheer me all the while.

4. Take the world, but give me Jesus;
In His Cross my trust shall be,
Till, with clearer, brighter vision,
Face to face my Lord I see.

## 169

My God I have found
The thrice blessed ground,
Where life, and where joy, and true comfort abound.

Cho—Hallelujah! thine the glory!
Hallelujah! amen!
Hallelujah! thine the glory!
Revive us again.

2. 'Tis found in the blood
Of him who once stood
My refuge and safety, my surety with God.

3. He bore on the tree
The sentence for me,
And now both the surety and sinner are free.

4. And though here below
'Mid sorrow and woe,
My place is in heaven with Jesus I know.

5. And this I shall find,
For such is his mind,
"He'll not be in glory and leave me behind."

## No. 170.
## HEAVEN WHISPERS.

Arr. by GEO. L. BROWN.

## No. 172
# HOW FIRM A FOUNDATION.

1. How firm a foun-da-tion, ye saints of the Lord, Is laid for your faith in His ex-cel-lent word! What more can He say to you than He hath said, You who un-to Je-sus for ref-uge have fled?
2. In ev'-ry con-di-tion, in sick-ness, in health, In pov-er-ty's vale, or a-bound-ing in wealth; At home and a-broad, on the land, on the sea, As your days may de-mand, shall your strength ev-er be.
3. E'en down to old age, all my peo-ple shall prove My sov'-reign, e-ter-nal, un-change-a-ble love; And when hoar-y hairs shall their tem-ples a-dorn, Like lambs they shall still in my bo-som be borne.
4. The soul that on Je-sus hath leaned for re-pose, I will not, I will not de-sert to its foes; That soul, though all hell should en-deav-or to shake, I'll nev-er, no, nev-er, no, nev-er for-sake!

## 173

There's a highway for the ransomed
  Where the children of the King,
Upon their pilgrim journey
  Triumphantly may sing,
Of a Savior who redeemed them,
  And delivers from all sin,
His blood now makes me clean.

Cho—Glory, glory, hallelujah!
  Glory, glory, hallelujah!
  Glory, glory, hallelujah!
  His blood now keeps me clean.

2 I was pardoned by God's mercy,
  But my heart was evil still,
A carnal mind was in me,
  Which resolves could never kill.
But, blessed be his holy name,
  He changes heart and will!
His blood now makes me clean.

3 Now, like pebbles in the running brook
  That 'neath the ripples lay,
My heart is sweetly kept from sin
  Each moment night and day;
And as faith the conquest gave me,
  I bid doubts to go their way,
His blood now makes me clean!

4 On the mountain tops of Beulah,
  Or in the vale below,
Where temptations' wildest hurricanes
  Their fiercest tempests blow,
In sorrow or in conflict
  His grace he doth bestow,
His blood now makes me clean!

5 He that dwelleth in the covert
  Of the highest of the high,
Abides in perfect safety
  And the devil's hosts defy,
As 'neath Jehovah's mighty wings
  No evil can come nigh,
His blood now makes me clean.

6 As the past I can't live over,
  Nor insure the coming years,
I claim the now salvation—
  Nor live in future fears;
Cross no bridges till I reach them,
  And shed no borrowed tears,
His blood now makes me clean.

## 174

Mine eyes have seen the glory,
  Of the coming of the Lord,
He is trampling out the vintage
  Where the grapes of wrath are stored;
He hath loosed the fateful lightning
  Of His terrible swift sword;
His truth is marching on.

2 I have seen Him in the watchfires
  Of a hundred circling camps;
They have builded Him an altar
  In the evening dews and damps;
I can read his righteous sentence
  By the dim and flaring lamps;
His day is marching on.

3 He has sounded forth the trumpet
  That shall never call retreat;
He is sifting out the hearts of men
  Before His judgment seat;
Oh, be swift, my soul, to answer Him!
  Be jubilant, my feet!
Our God is marching on.

## 175

Tune—"Glory, hallelujah."

On the mountain top of vision
  What a glory we behold,
A hundred years of victory
  Are tinging earth with gold,
And the glorious time is coming
  Which the prophets long foretold,
The truth is marching on.

Cho—Glory, &c.

2 For the glory of the Master
  Wesley taught beyond the sea,
And preached the full salvation
  Which delivers you and me;
And a million voices shout it,—
  "Redemption's full and free,"
Salvation's marching on.

3 From the cabin on the prairie,
  From the vaulted city doom,
From the dark and briny ocean
  Where our sailor brothers roam,
We hear the glad rejoicing,
  Like a happy harvest home,
Salvation's rolling on.

4 A hundred years of marching
  And a hundred years of song,
The Conqueror advances
  And the time will not be long,
When He shall claim the heathen
  And over throw the wrong,
Our God is marching on.

5 And when the war is over
  With the saints forever more,
On the blissful heights of glory
  We will shout the battle o'er,
And in the golden city
  We will join the Conqueror,
Forever marching on.

## 176

I have entered the valley of blessing so sweet,
  And Jesus abides with me there;
And his spirit and blood makes my cleansing complete,
  And his perfect love casteth out fear.

Chorus.

O come to this valley of blessing so sweet,
  Where Jesus will fulness bestow,
And believe, and receive, and confess him,
  That all his salvation may know.

2 There is peace in the valley of blessing so sweet,
  And plenty the land doth impart;
And there's rest for the weary, worn traveler's feet,
  And joy for the sorrowing heart.

3 There is love in the valley of blessing so sweet,
  Such as none but the blood-washed may feel;
When heaven comes down redeemed spirits to greet,
  And Christ sets his covenant seal.

4 There's a song in the valley of blessing so sweet,
  That angels would fain join the strain;
As with rapturous praise we bow at his feet,
  Crying worthy the Lamb that was slain.

## No. 177.
## A CHANGED HYMN.

Ind. Catholic Magazine.  GEO. L. BROWN.

## Highway Hymnal.

### 179

Ye who know your sins forgiven,
And are happy in the Lord,
Have you read the gracious promise
Which is left upon record?
I will sprinkle you with water,
I will cleanse you from all sin.
Sanctify and make you holy;
I will come and dwell within.

CHO—Then palms of victory, crowns of glory,
Palms of victory I shall wear.

2 Though you have much peace and comfort,
Greater things you yet may find;
Freedom from unholy tempers,
Freedom from the carnal mind,
To procure your full salvation.
Jesus suffer'd, groan'd, and died
On the cross: the healing fountain
Gushed from the wounded side.

3 Come, ye hungry, thirsty children,
Seek, O seek, this holy state;
None but holy ones can enter
Through the pure celestial gate,
Can you bear the thought of losing
All the joys that are above?
When, by simple faith in Jesus,
You may know his perfect love.

4 Be as holy and as happy,
And as useful here below,
As it is your father's pleasure,—
Jesus only Jesus know.
Spread, O spread the holy fire,
Meekly tell what God has done;
Till all nations are conformed
To the image of his Son.

5 O ye tender babes in Jesus,
Hear your heavenly Father's will,
Claim your portion plead his promise,
And he quickly will fulfill,—
Pray, and the refining fire
Will come streaming from above,—
Now believe and gain the blessing,
Nothing less than perfect love.

6 If you have obtained the treasure,
Search and you shall surely find
All the Christian marks and graces
Planted, growing in your mind,
Perfect faith and perfect patience,
Perfect lowliness and then
Perfect hope and perfect meekness,
Perfect love for God and man.

7 But be sure to gain the witness
Which abides both day and night;
This your God has plainly promised,
This is like a stream of light,
While you keep the blessed witness
All is clear and calm within;
God himself assures you by it,
That your heart is cleansed from sin.

8 Witnesses might be produced
Of this glorious work of love,
Paul and James, and John and Peter,
Long before they went above,
Hundreds, thousands, tens of thousands,
Have, and do, and will appear,
Let me ask a solemn question,
Has the Lord a witness here?

9 Rouse up, Brother, rouse up, Sister,
Seek, O seek, this holy state,
None but holy ones can enter,
Through the pure celestial gate,
Can you bear the thought of losing
All the joys that are above?
No, my brother, no, my sister,
God will perfect you in love.

10 May a mighty sound from heaven,
Suddenly come rushing down,
Cloven tongues like us of fire,
May they set on all around,
O may every soul be filled
With the Holy Ghost to-day;
It is coming, it is coming,
O prepare, prepare the way.

### 180

From "Revivalist."

I will follow thee, my Saviour,
Wherso'er my lot may be;
Where thou goest, I will follow,
Yes, my Lord, I'll follow thee.

CHO—I will follow thee, my Saviour;
Thou didst shed thy blood for me;
And tho' all men should forsake thee,
By thy grace I'll follow thee.

2 Tho' the road be rough and thorny,
Trackless as the foaming sea,
Thou hast trod this way before me,
And I gladly follow thee.

3 Tho' 'tis lone, and dark, and dreary,
Cheerless though my path may be,
If thy voice I hear before me,
Fearlessly I'll follow thee.

4 Tho' I meet with tribulations,
Sorely tempted though I be,
I remember thou wast tempted,
And rejoice to follow thee.

5 Tho' thou leadest me thro' affliction,
Poor, forsaken, though I be;
Thou wast destitute, afflicted,
And I only follow thee.

6 Tho' to Jordan's rolling billows,
Cold and deep thou bid'st me;
Thou hast cross'd its waves before me,
And I still will follow thee.

### 181

Should the death angel knock at thy chamber
In the still watch of the night;
Say, would thy spirit pass into torment
Or to the realms of delight?

CHO—Say are you ready, O are you ready
If the death angel should call?
Say are you ready, O are you ready?
Jesus stands pleading for all.

2 Many sad spirits now are descending
Into the world of despair,
Every brief moment brings your doom nearer,
Sinner, O, sinner beware.

3 Many redeemed ones now are ascending
Into the mansions of light,
Jesus is pleading high up in glory,
Seeking to save you to-night.

## 182

Gems of Gospel Song. Enlarged by M. E. S.

Sowing in the morning, sowing seeds of kindness,
Sowing in the noon tide and the dewy eve;
Waiting for the harvest, and the time of reaping,
We shall come rejoicing, bringing in the sheaves.

CHORUS.

Bringing in the sheaves, bringing in the sheaves,
We shall come rejoicing, bringing in the sheaves.

2 Sowing in the sunshine, sowing in the shadows
Fearing neither clouds, nor winter's chilling breeze;
By and by the harvest, and the labors ended,
We shall come rejoicing, bringing in the sheaves.

3 Go and tell the nations now in heathen blindness,
Tell them that Jesus died, now no excuse he leaves,
Bid them come to Jesus, thus prepare the harvest,
You shall come rejoicing, bringing in the sheaves.

4 Go then, even weeping, sowing for the Master,
Though the loss sustained, our spirit often grieves;
When our weeping's over, he will bid us welcome;
We shall come rejoicing, bringing in the sheaves.

## 183

Enlarged and Re-arranged for Highway Hymns.

Jesus, my Saviour, to Bethlehem came,
Born in a manger to sorrow and shame;
Oh, it was wonderful, blest be his name,
    Seeking for me, for me,
    Seeking for me, for me,
    Seeking for me, for me;
Oh, it was wonderful, blest be his name,
    Seeking for me, for me.

2 Jesus, my Saviour, on Calvary's tree,
Paid the great debt, and my soul he set free;
Oh, it was wonderful, how could it be?
    Dying for me, for me,
    Dying for me, for me,
    Dying for me, for me;
Oh, it was wonderful, how could it be?
    Dying for me, for me.

3 Jesus, my Saviour, the same as of old,
While I did wander afar from the fold,
Gently and long he hath plead with my soul,
    Calling for me, for me,
    Calling for me, for me,
    Calling for me, for me;
Gently and long he hath plead with my soul,
    Calling for me, for me.

4 Jesus, my Saviour, the sweetest of all,
Has come to his temple, possessing the whole;
Oh, I do see him, the fairest of all,
    Abiding in me, in me,
    Abiding in me, in me,
    Abiding in me, in me,
Oh, I do see him, the fairest of all,
    Abiding in me, in me.

5 Jesus, my Saviour, shall come from on high,
Sweet is the promise, as weary years fly;
Oh, I shall see him descending the sky,
    Coming for me, for me,
    Coming for me, for me,
    Coming for me, for me;
Oh, I shall see him descending the sky,
    Coming for me, for me.

## 184

From "Songs of Triumph."

O sometimes the shadows are deep,
    And rough seems the path to the goal,
And sorrows, sometime how they sweep
    Like tempests down over the soul.

CHO—O, then, to the Rock let me fly,
    To the Rock that is higher than I;
    O, then, to the Rock let me fly,
    To the Rock that is higher than I.

2 O, sometimes, how long seems the day,
    And sometimes how weary my feet,
But toiling in life's dusty way,
    The Rock's blessed shadow how sweet!

3 O, near to the Rock let me keep,
    Or blessings, or sorrows prevail;
Or climbing the mountain way steep,
    Or walking the shadowy vale.

## 185

From "Revivalist."

What poor despised company
    Of travellers are these,
Who walk in yonder narrow way,
    Along that rugged maze?

CHO—O I'd rather be the least of them,
    Who are the Lord's alone,
Than wear a royal diadem,
    And sit upon a throne.

2 Ah! these are of a royal line,
    All children of a King,
Heirs of immortal crowns divine,
    And lo! for joy they sing.

3 Why then do they appear so mean?
    And why so much despised?
Because of their rich robes unseen,
    The world is not apprised.

4 But some of them seem poor, distressed,
    And lacking daily bread,
Ah! they're of boundless wealth possess'd,
    With heavenly manna fed.

5 Why do they shun the pleasing path,
    That worldlings love so well?
Because it is the way to death,
    The open road to hell.

6 But why keep they the narrow road,
    That rugged thorny maze?
Why that's the way their Saviour trod,
    They love to keep his ways.

7 What! is there then no other road
    To Salem's happy ground?
Christ is the only way to God,
    None other can be found.

## THE EDEN ABOVE.

R. L. COLLIER.

1. We're bound for the land of the pure and the ho-ly,
Ye wand'-rers from God, in the broad road of fol-ly,
The home of the hap-py, the king-dom of love;
O say, will you go to the E-den a-bove?
Will you go, Will you go, Will you go, Will you go?
O say, will you go to the E-den a-bove?

2 In that blessed land neither sighing nor anguish,
Can breathe in the fields where the glorified move,
Ye heart-burdened ones, who in misery languish,
O say, will you go to the Eden above?
Will you go, etc.

3 Nor fraud, nor deceit, nor the hand of oppression,
Can injure the dwellers in that holy grove;
No wickedness there, not a shade of transgression,
O say, will you go to the Eden above?
Will you go, etc.

4 No poverty there—no, the saints are all wealthy,
The heirs of his glory whose nature is love;
Nor sickness can reach them, that country is healthy,
O say, will you go to the Eden above?
Will you go, etc.

5 Each saint has a mansion prepared and all furnished,
Ere from this clay house he is summoned to move;
Its gates and its towers with glory are burnished,
O say, will you go to the Eden above?
Will you go, etc.

6 March on, happy pilgrims, that land is before you,
And soon its ten thousand delights we shall prove,
Yes, soon we shall walk o'er the hill of bright glory,
And drink the pure joys of the Eden above.
We will go, we will go,
O yes, we will go to the Eden above.

7 And yet, guilty sinner, we would not forsake thee,
We halt yet a moment as onward we move;
O come to thy Lord, in his arms he will take thee,
And bear thee along to the Eden above.
Will you go, Will you go,
O say, will you go to the Eden above?

8 Methinks thou art now in thy wretchedness saying,
O, who can this guilt from my conscience remove?
No other but Jesus; then come to him praying,
Prepare me, O Lord, for the Eden above,
Will you go, Will you go,
At last, will you go to the Eden above?

## No 187

Thou my everlasting portion,
More than friend or life to me,
All along my pilgrim journey
Saviour, let me walk with Thee.

REF—Close to thee, close to thee,
Close to thee, close to thee,
All along my pilgrim journey,
Saviour let me walk with thee.

2 Not for ease or worldly pleasure,
Nor for fame my prayer shall be;
Gladly will I toil and suffer,
Only let me walk with thee.

REF—Close to thee, close to thee,
Close to thee, close to thee;
Gladly will I toil and suffer,
Only let me walk with thee.

3 Lead me thro' the vale of shadows,
Bear me o'er life's fitful sea;
Then the gate of life eternal,
May I enter, Lord, with thee.

REF—Close to thee, close to thee;
Close to thee, close to thee;
Then the gate of life eternal,
May I enter, Lord, with thee.

## No. 188
# WE'LL GIVE THE GLORY TO JESUS.
*Arranged by GEO. L. BROWN.*

1. I love the Lord, I know I do, I'll dwell in his love, I'll dwell in his love; I'll praise him for-ev-er-more.
   The best of all he loves me, too,

CHO.—We'll give the glo-ry to Je-sus, And dwell in his love, And dwell in his love; And praise him for-ev-er-more.
We'll give the glo-ry to Je-sus,

2 I am a soldier of the cross,
Nor will I fear to own his cause.

3 Sure, I must fight if I would reign,
I'll bear the toil, endure the pain.

4 Forever here my rest shall be,
His blood is all my hope and plea.

5 He breaks the power of cancelled sin,
He cleanses me and keeps me clean.

6 Oh, praise the Lord, his sacred fire
Burns up the dross of base desire.

7 The consecrated cross I'll bear,
And then go home a crown to wear.

## 189

Alas! and did my Savior bleed,
And did my Sovereign die?
Would he devote that sacred head
For such a worm as I?

CHO—IO, how I love Jesus:I
Because he first loved me.

2 Was it for crimes that I had done
He groaned upon the tree?
Amazing pity! grace unknown!
And love beyond degree.

3 Well might the sun in darkness hide,
And shut his glories in,
When Christ, the mighty Maker, died
For man, the creature's sin.

4 Thus might I hide my blushing face,
While his dear cross appears,
Dissolve my heart in thankfulness,
And melt mine eyes to tears.

5 But drops of grief can ne'er repay
The debt of love I owe;
Here, Lord, I give myself away;
'Tis all that I can do.

## 190

*From "Beulah Songs."*

In the rifted rock I'm resting,
Safely shelter'd I abide,
There no foes no storms molest me,
While within the cleft I hide.

CHO—Now I'm resting, sweetly resting,
In the cleft once made for me;
Jesus blessed Rock of Ages,
I will hide myself in thee.

2 Long pursued by sin and Satan,
Weary, sad, I long'd for rest;
Then I found this heav'nly shelter,
Open'd in my Saviour's breast.

3 Peace, which passeth understanding,
Joy, the world can never give,
Now in Jesus I am finding;
In his smiles of love I live.

4 In the Rifted Rock I'll hide me,
Till the storms of life are past,
All secure in this blest refuge,
Heeding not the fiercest blast.

Lord, I am thine, entirely thine,
Purchased and saved by blood divine;
With full consent thine would I be,
And own thy sovereign right in me.

2 Thine would I live, thine would I die,
Be thine through all eternity;
The vow is passed, beyond repeal,
And now I set the solemn seal.

3 Here at the cross where flows the blood,
That bought my guilty soul for God,
Thee, my new Master, now, I call,
And consecrate to thee my all.

## 193

I am the vine and ye are the branches,
Bear precious fruit for Jesus to-day.
The branch that in me no fruit ever beareth
Jesus hath said, He taketh away.

CHORUS.

I am the vine and ye are the branches,
I am the vine, be faithful and true,
Ask what ye will, your prayer shall be granted.
The Father lov'd me so I have lov'd you.

2 Now ye are clean through words I have spoken;
Abiding in me much fruit ye shall bear,
Dwelling in thee my promise unbroken,
Glory with me in Heaven ye shall share.

3 Yes, by your fruit the world is to know you;
Walking in love as children of day;
Follow your guide, He has pass'd on before you,
Bidding to realms of glorious day.

## 194

1 Bless'd are the pure in heart
For they shall see our God,
The secret of the Lord is their s,
Their soul is Christ's abode.

2 The Lord, who left the heavens,
Our life and peace to bring,
To dwell in lowliness with men
Their Pattern and their King.

3 He to the lowly soul
Doth still himself impart,
And for His dwelling and His throne
Chooseth the pure in heart.

4 Lord, we thy presence seek,
May ours this blessing be,
Give us a pure and lowly heart
A temple meet for Thee.

5 By faith we enter now—
We plunge beneath the wave,
Whose waters wash us white as snow
And sanctify and save.

[First four stanzas selected.

## 195

The voice of the Lord sweetly sayeth to me,
The true vine am I and the branches are ye,
Abide ye in me, all ye branches of mine,
Abide, O abide, in the true living vine.

CHORUS.

Lovely Vine, let thy life thro' us flow,
No life out of thee can we know,
Oh love all divine flowing ever thro' the vine,
In thee will the branches ever grow.

2 Thou Father all holy the husbandman art,
The branch without fruit will thy hand take away,
O, all seeing eye rather purge thou my heart,
Nor let me, dear Lord, from thee e'er go astray

3 Much fruit may we bear to thy glory, O Lord,
As upward we grow through the vine unto thee,
Abiding in love and obeying thy word,
Thy branches forever and ever to be.

## 196

On the carnal field of mammon
Where Apollyon's army lay,
And the servile hosts of Agar,
Are in battle, full array.
We a little band of Christians,
All their forces dare to meet;
For we're sounding forth the trumpet
That shall never call retreat.

CHO—No, never call retreat,
No, never call retreat,
We are sounding forth the trumpet,
That shall never call retreat.

2 We have raised the gospel banner,
With its standard planted high;
And through Jesus, our Redeemer,
We shall conquer though we die.
All the art of holy fighting
We will learn at Jesus' feet,
Who has bid us sound the trumpet
That shall never call retreat.

3 We have drawn the sword for glory,
And the scabbard thrown away,
We have buckled on our armor
And are sure to win the day.
With our head beneath the helmet,
And the Rock beneath our feet,
We are sounding forth the trumpet,
That shall never call retreat.

4 This we'll do until victorious
Over Satan, death and sin,
Then with joy and final triumph
Shall forever enter in,
To the city where the angels
And the ransomed hosts will meet,
Who have sounded forth the trumpet.
That did never call retreat.

## 197

From "Revivalist."

I'm a pilgrim and a stranger passing over,
The road may be rough, but 'tis clear,
And a starry crown awaits me o'er the river,
And Jesus bids me welcome there.

CHORUS.

There are lights along the shore that never grow dim,
That never, never grow dim;
These souls are all aflame with the love of Jesus' name,
They guide us, yes, they guide us unto him.

2 Sometimes I meet with trials on my journey.
Temptation and sorrow by the way;
But Jesus speaks, and says "I'm ever near thee,
To guide to realms of endless day."

3 Friends of Jesus! may you lights be trimm'd and burning,
And shining along the way of love;
Soon you'll gain the heights of glory, and be singing
The happy songs of saints above.

4 We're a happy band of Christians, bound for Canaan,
The land is in view, the wind's fair;
We will sing redeeming love beyond the Jordan,
With Jesus dwell forever there

## 198
Tune—"Nellie Gray."

1 I have long been a traveler along life's rugg-
  ed road,
  And have had many trials by the way;
  But each conflict always brings me nearer
  to the throne of God.
  And the joys in those realms of endless day.

CHORUS.

Oh! in that blessed mansion, where he's gone
  to make me room
I shall never have sorrow any more.
I am waiting, waiting, waiting, till the Lord
  shall call me home;
Then with joy I shall leave this weary shore.

2 The more the world oppose me, as I journey
   on my way,
  And try to allure me from the right,
  I pay the less attention to anything they say
  And onward I journey with my might.

3 They often try to stop me, and invite me to
   go in,
  And enjoy their pleasures by the way;
  But my time is very precious, and I'm not in-
   clined to sin,
  Or for any of their trifles here to stay.

4 I have all sold out to Jesus, and no longer
   am my own,
  For I'm bought with his own precious blood,
  And my business is to journey till he gives me
   the crown,
  And I gain the bright city of my God.

5 Every day I'm getting nearer to my happy
   home above,
  For the light shines brighter on my way;
  And my soul is rising higher as it's filled with
   joy and love,
  As it nears the world of endless day.

6 Sometimes, in my visions, my troubles are
   all gone,
  When faith's eye is clear as the sun,
  I see the streaming glory, and I hear redemp-
   tion's song,
  And I think that the angels sure have come.

7 Now I'm waiting on the mountain, where
   Moses once did stand,
  And I listen to the music from that shore;
  I am waiting for the summons from my dear
   Redeemer's hand,
  To cross over and abide forever more.

## 199
Tune—"Will you Meet me at the Fountain?"

I have found the richest treasure
  That a soul could ever know,
Found it by the cross of Jesus,
  Found it where the blood does flow.
How my heart was longing, longing,
  For the fulness from above,
And my soul was thirsting, thirsting,
  For the riches of his love!

CHORUS.

Now I'm resting, sweetly resting,
  Underneath the crimson flow;
And the blood is cleansing, cleansing,
  Making me as "white as snow."

2 Through Gethsemane he led me,
  Then to Calvary's mountain side,
  And, upon the cross of Jesus,
  I with Christ am crucified.
  Now I'm walking in his footsteps,
  Dead I am to self and sin,
  And a flood of wondrous glory,
  Sweetly fills my soul within.

3 Now my all is on the altar,
  I do now in Christ abide,
  A living sacrifice to Jesus—
  Thus my soul is satisfied,
  How he fills me with his power!
  Oh, the wonders of his love!
  I am drinking of life's river,
  Flowing from the throne above.
                                  F. E. L.

## 200
Rev. L. Hartsough, with per.

"I bring you tidings of great joy,"
  For Jesus comes to save his own
Yes, Jesus comes, tho' Lord of all,
  For you he leaves his heavenly home.

CHORUS.

Rejoice, his name is Jesus, for he saves;
Rejoice, his name is Jesus, for he saves.
For he saves, for he saves,
For he saves his people from their sins.

2 Just at the door with lifted hand,
  He stands and knocks—would enter in;
  Who welcomes Christ with heart and soul,
  Will prove that Jesus saves from sin.

3 No other friend can bless us,
  You've greeted others—welcome him;
  What foes you've had—you thought them
   friends,
  Jesus, true friend, will save from sin.

4 Besetting sins to Christ will yield,
  Through him all self will find a grave;
  And all this deadly strife will cease,
  As Jesus proves his power to save.

5 And purity is his free gift,
  Thus saving to the uttermost;
  And by the Holy Spirit's power,
  He gives to us our Pentecost.

## 201

The judgment day is coming, coming, com-
 ing,
The judgment day is coming;
O, that great day!

CHO—Let us take the wings of the morning,
  And fly away to Jesus,
  Let us take the wings of the morning,
  And sound the jubilee.

2 I hear the trumpet sounding, sounding,
   I hear the trumpet sounding,
  O, that great day!

3 I hear the thunder rolling, &c.

4 I see the lightning flashing, &c.

5 I see the stars a falling, &c.

6 I see the dead arising, &c.

7 I hear the righteous shouting, &c.

8 I hear the wicked wailing, &c.

## 202

Awake, my soul, in joyful lays,
And sing my great Redeemer's praise,
He justly claims a song from me—
His loving-kindness, Oh, how free!

2 He saw me ruined by the fall,
Yet loved me, notwithstanding all;
He saved me from my lost estate—
His loving-kindness, Oh, how great!

3 Through numerous hosts of mighty foes,
Though earth and hell my way oppose,
He safely leads my soul along—
His loving-kindness, Oh, how strong!

4 When trouble, like a gloomy cloud,
Has gathered thick and thundered loud,
He near my soul has always stood—
His loving-kindness, Oh, how good!

5 Soon shall I pass the gloomy vale,
Soon all my mortal powers must fail;
Oh! may my last expiring breath
His loving-kindness sing in death!

## 203

And can it be that I should gain
An interest in the Saviour's blood?
Died he for me, who caused his pain?
For me, who him to death pursued?
‖Amazing love! how can it be,
That thou, my Lord, shouldst die for me?‖

2 'Tis myst'ry all—th' Immortal dies!
Who can explore his strange design?
In vain the first-born seraph tries
To sound the depths of love divine;
‖'Tis mercy all! let earth adore:
Let angel minds inquire no more.‖

3 He left his Father's throne above;
(So free, so infinite his grace!)
Emptied himself of all but love,
And bled for Adam's helpless race;
‖'Tis mercy all, immense and free,
For, O my God, it found out me!‖

4 Long my imprisoned spirit lay,
Fast bound in sin and nature's night;
Thine eye diffused a quickening ray;
I woke; the dungeon flamed with light;
‖My chains fell off, my heart was free—
I rose, went forth, and followed thee.‖

5 No condemnation now I dread—
Jesus, with all in him, is mine;
Alive in him, my living head,
And clothed in righteousness divine,
‖Bold I approach th' eternal throne,
And claim the crown, through Christ, my own.‖

## 204

"Songs of Triumph," with per.

O, I left it all with Jesus long ago, long ago,
My sinfulness I brought Him and my woe,
And when by faith I saw him on the tree,
And heard His still small whisper, " 'tis for thee,"
From my weary heart the burden rolled away, rolled away,
And now I'm singing glory, happy day.

2 O, I leave it all with Jesus, for He knows, for He knows,
Just how to take the bitter from life's woes,
And how to gild the tear-drop with His smile,
To make the desert garden bloom awhile,
Then, with all my weakness leaning on His might, on His might,
My soul sings hallelujah, all is light.

3 O, I leave it all with Jesus day by day, day by day,
My faith can firmly trust Him, come what may,
For hope has dropped her anchor, found her rest,
Within the calm sure haven of His breast,
And oh! 'tis joy of heaven to abide, to abide,
Close to my dear Redeemer at His side.

## 205

Tune—"Rock of Ages."

Every boon that heaven can grant,
Every grace my soul can want,
All are merited by thee,
Blood of Christ, so rich and free,
Likeness lost in Adam's fall,
Jesus' blood has bought it all.

2 Jesus saves me when I lay
In the pit and miry clay,
Power that lifted from the deep,
Surely on the rock can keep,
While I trust the living word,
Thou wilt do the keeping, Lord.

3 Thy sweet will and mine agree,
Sanctified I want to be;
Do what thou hast died to do,
Cleanse my nature thro' and thro',
Trustingly, I take from Thee,
Purchased, promised purity.

4 Till He loses heaven's throne,
Till His faithfulness is gone,
On the Altar I'll abide,
Trusting, resting, sanctified.
Mine this moment, mine by faith,
All the glorious promise saith.
MANIE PAYNE.

## 206

Tune, 132.

How happy every child of grace,
Who knows his sins forgiven!
This earth, he cries, is not my place
I seek my place in heaven.

2 A country far from mortal sight,
Yet, O, by faith I see;
The land of rest, the saints' delight,—
The heaven prepared for me.

3 O, what a blessed hope is ours!
While here on earth we stay,
We more than taste the heav'nly pow'rs,
And antedate that day.

4 We feel the resurrection near,—
Our life in Christ concealed,—
And with his glorious presence here
Our earthen vessel's filled.

5 O, what are all our sufferings here;
If, Lord thou count me meet,
With that enraptured host to appear,
And worship at thy feet.

6 Give joy or grief, give ease or pain,
Take life or friends away,
But let me find them all again
In that eternal day.

## HIGHWAY HYMNAL.

### 207

1 Just as I am without one plea,
But that thy blood was shed for me,
And that thou bidst me come to thee,
O Lamb of God! I come, I come!

2 Just as I am, and waiting not
To rid my soul of one dark blot,
To thee, whose blood can cleanse each spot,
O Lamb of God! I come, I come!

3 Just as I am, poor, wretched, blind,
Sight, riches, healing of the mind,
Yea, all I need, in thee to find,
O Lamb of God! I come, I come!

4 Just as I am; thou wilt receive,
Wilt welcome, pardon, cleanse, relieve;
Because thy promise I believe,
O Lamb of God! I come, I come!

5 Just as I am—thy love I own,
Has broken every barrier down;
Now, to be thine, yea, thine alone,
O Lamb of God! I come! I come!

### 208

1 I know I'm trusting Jesus, I know I'm trusting Jesus,
I know I'm trusting Jesus, He saves me now.

CHORUS—Low down at the feet of Jesus,
Low down at the feet of Jesus,
Low down at the feet of Jesus,
He saves me now.

2 I know that Jesus saves me, I know that Jesus saves me,
I know that Jesus saves me, he saves me now.

3 I'm at the fountain drinking, I'm at the fountain drinking,
I'm at the fountain drinking, he saves me now.

4 I feel the fire now burning, I feel the fire now burning,
I feel the fire now burning, He saves me now.

### 209

From "Joy to the World."

Christ in me the hope for all,
While he leads I cannot fall;
Be I low, or lifted up,
Jesus sweetens every cup.

CHO—Jesus all the way along,
Jesus is my prayer and song,
Jesus gives a peace sublime,
Jesus, Jesus all the time.

2 Though myself am e'er so frail,
Christ my Saviour ne'er can fail,
While he lives and reigns in me,
Sure my anchorage must be,

3 Jesus reigns, all fulness dwells,
Every cloud of doubt dispels;
If I in the valley stay
Jesus brightens all the way.

4 What an easy quiet road,
Traveling on to Heaven and God;
Trusting Him, he knoweth best—
Here is where I find my rest.

5 Jesus every day and hour,
Jesus keeps with mighty power;
Oh the preciousness to be
Just relying, Lord, on thee.

### 210

TUNE—"Bower of Prayer."

1 God's car of salvation is now passing by,
Oh who'll go a pilgrimage home to the sky?
Ye wretched, ye needy, ye lame and ye blind,
A right hearty welcome on board you will find.

2 The blessed Conductor will help you on board,
And gracious assistance and comfort afford,
He'll see to your baggage that nothing be lost,
And grant a through passage without price or cost.

3 But see that your treasures are every one given
To the blessed Conductor and laid up in heaven,
For you and your treasures at whatever cost,
Must all go together—be saved or be lost.

4 O come, weary waiting one, take the first train,
For daylight is passing, and night comes again;
No time to turn homeward to bid friends adieu,
All heaven is waiting to see this train through.

5 This train has no depot or station up town,
No worldly-wise persons of fame or renown
Have ever been willing to leave their abode
And travel, with pilgrims, this cross-bearing road.

6 But down by the highways and hedges beside,
Where the wretched and poor and needy abide,
'Tis there this train pauses and takes her supplies
Of pilgrims en route for their home in the skies.

7 No room for dame fashion, for ruffles and curls,
No worldly adorning—gold, silver or pearls;
No room for earth's pleasures, church picnics or sprees,
E'en though the poor preacher does pocket the fees.

8 Then onward, right onward, past traffic and trash,
Past robbers and merchantmen scrambling for cash;
Past tall steepled churches and all rented pews,
And loud-sounding organs and close-fisted Jews.

9 No room for indulgence in any known sin,
In snuff or tobacco, in brandy or gin;
No room for a Mason, Odd Fellow or Knight,
Who's walking in darkness and calling it light.

10 No running to Egypt for barley and corn,
But running to heaven through tempest and storm.
On, on through the conflict, the din and the strife,
On, on to the evergreen mountains of life.

## No. 211.
### THE OLD ISRAELITES. 12s & 9s.

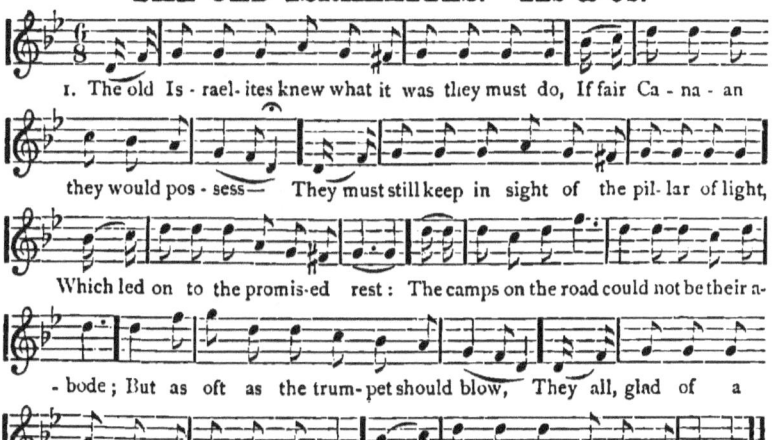

1. The old Is-rael-ites knew what it was they must do, If fair Ca-na-an they would pos-sess— They must still keep in sight of the pil-lar of light, Which led on to the promis-ed rest: The camps on the road could not be their a-bode; But as oft as the trum-pet should blow, They all, glad of a chance of a fur-ther ad-vance, Must then take up their baggage and go.

2 I am thankful indeed for the Heavenly Head,
Which before me has hitherto gone;
For that pillar of Love which doth onward still move
And doth gather our souls into one.
Now the cross bearing throng, are advancing along,
And a closer communion doth flow;
Now all who would stand on the promised land,
Let them take up their crosses and go.

3 The way is all new, as it opens to view,
And behind is the foaming Red Sea;
So none need to speak of the onions and leeks,
Or to talk about garlics to me;
On Jordan's near side I can never abide;
For no place here of refuge I see,
Till I come to the spot, and inherit the lot
Which the Lord God will give unto me.

4 What though some in the rear preach up terror and fear,
And complain of the trials they meet?
Though the giants before with great fury do roar
I'm resolved I will never retreat.

We are little, 'tis true, and our numbers are few,
And the sons of old Anak are tall;
But while I see a track, I will never go back,
But go on at the risk of my all.

5 Now the bright morning dawns for the camps to move on,
And the priests with their trumpets do blow;
As the priests give the sound and the trumpets resound,
All my soul is exulting to go.
If I'm faithful and true, and my journey pursue
Till I stand on the heavenly shore,
I shall joyfully see, what a blessing to me,
Was the mortifying cross which I bore.

6 All my honors and wealth, all my pleasures and health,
I am willing should now be at stake;
If my Christ I obtain, I shall think it great gain,
For the sacrifice which I shall make;
When I all have forsook, like a bubble 'twill look,
From the midst of the glorified throng,
Where all losses are gain, where each sorrow and pain
Are exchanged for the conqueror's song.

### 212

Take the name of Jesus with you,
On your journey here below,
It will joy and comfort give you,
Take it then where'er you go.

Cho—Precious name, O how sweet!
Hope of earth and joy of heaven,
Precious name, O how sweet—
Hope of earth and joy of heaven.

2 Take the name of Jesus ever,
As a shield from every snare;
If temptations round you gather,
Breathe that holy name in prayer.

3 Oh! the precious name of Jesus!
How it thrills our souls with joy,
When his loving arms receive us,
And his songs our tongues employ!

4 At the name of Jesus bowing,
Falling prostrate at his feet,
King of kings in heav'n we'll crown him,
When our journey is complete.

## No. 213.
## THE SUN-BRIGHT CLIME.
Rev. W. F. FARRINGTON.

Have you heard? have you heard of the sun-bright clime, Undimm'd by sorrow, unhurt by time; Where age has no power o'er the fadeless frame; Where the eye is fire and the heart is flame, Have you heard of that sun-bright clime?

2 A river of water gushes there,
'Mid flowers of beauty, strangely fair,
And a thousand wings are hovering o'er
The dazzling waves and the golden shore
That are seen in that sun-bright clime.

3 Millions of forms, all clothed in light,
In garments of beauty, clean and white,
They dwell in their own immortal bowers,
'Mid fadeless hues of countless flowers
That bloom in that sun-bright clime.

4 Ear hath not heard, and eye hath not seen,
Their swelling songs or their changeless sheen;
There ensigns are waving, and banners unfurl
O'er jasper walls, and gates of pearl,
That are fixed in that sun-bright clime.

5 But far away is that sun-bright clime,
Undimmed by sorrow, unhurt by time,
There amid all things that are fair is given,
The home of the saved, and its name is heaven,
The name of the sun-bright clime.

ADDITIONAL VERSES FROM "DR. REDFIELD'S DREAM."

6 But far, far above that countless throng
I hear a wilder note of song.
'Twas out of great distress they came,
Washed in the blood of yonder Lamb,
Who reigns in that sun-bright clime.

7 Prophets, apostles, martyrs all,
From the lion's den—the prison stall—
From the Hebrew furnace' dreadful fire
Raised by the whirling tempest higher,
To dwell in that sun-bright clime.

8 Ten thousand, THOUSAND, THOUSAND more,
From every age, from every shore,
Who battle till the war is o'er,
With God shut in forevermore,
To reign in that sun-bright clime.

## No. 214.
Re-arranged. Do not sing it the old way.

How happy and joyful the hours,
As Jesus I constantly see,
As fragrance from heaven's own bowers
Has now such great sweetness to me!
Earth's pleasures to me are all dim;
The world strives in vain to look gay;
But since I am dead unto sin,
December's as pleasant as May.

2 His name yields the richest perfume,
And sweeter than music his voice;
His presence disperses my gloom,
And makes all within me rejoice;
Now while I'm abiding in Him,
I've nothing to wish or to fear;
I'm now dead indeed unto sin,
My summer now lasts all the year.

3 Content with the fulness of grace,
My all to his will is resigned;
No changes of season or place
Can make any change in my mind,
I'm blessed with the fulness of grace,
My heart is with gladness set free,
And prisons do palaces prove
While Jesus forever saves me.

4 My Lord, now indeed I am thine
And thou art my sun and my lay;
I never can languish and pine,
My sun shines so bright all the day;
The clouds are all gone from my sky;
I've op'ned the Master each door;
I'm waiting to soar up on high,
. With Jesus to dwell evermore.

## No. 215
## ROOM ENOUGH.

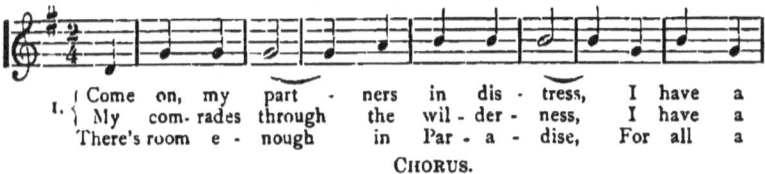

1. Come on, my partners in distress, I have a home in glory;
My comrades through the wilderness, I have a home in glory;
There's room enough in Paradise, For all a home in glory;

CHORUS.

O glory, O glory!

2 Beyond the bounds of time and space,
We have a home in glory;
Look forward to that heavenly place,
We have a home in glory.

3 Who suffer with our Master here
Shall have a home in glory;
And shall before his face appear,
We have a home in glory.

4 Our conflicts here shall soon be past,
We have a home in glory;
And you and I ascend at last,
We have a home in glory.

### 216
TUNE—"There's Room Enough."

Sweet bards may chant melodious lays,
And fame may tell the story,
I envy not their fading praise,
For I'm to sing in glory.

CHO— Oh glory! Oh glory!
There's room enough in Paradise,
For all a home in glory.

2 For heaps of gold let others toil,
Form blooming years to hoary,
Nor rust corrupt, nor thieves can spoil
My treasured home in glory.

3 No city have I here, nor home,
Where all is transitory,
But though on earth I homeless roam,
I have a home in glory.

4 When near the cross the Saviour stood,
He said: I go before you
A mansion to prepare, that you
May dwell with me in glory.

### 217

O, sinner, come without delay,
And seek a home in glory;
The Lord is calling you to-day,
He pleads for you in glory.

CHO—Oh, glory! Oh, glory!
There's room enough in Paradise,
For all a home in glory.

2 Sent by my Lord, on you I call,
To seek a home in glory;
The invitation is to all,
To have a home in glory.

3 Ye weary, heavy-laden, come,
And have a home in glory;
In yon blest house there still is room
For you a home in glory.

4 There need not one be left behind,
Who seek a home in glory;
For God hath bidden all mankind,
To have a home in glory.

5 Awake! awake! the Judge is near;
Prepare, prepare for glory!
If sleeping when he shall appear,
You cannot share his glory.

2d Cho—Oh, glory! Oh, glory!
There's power in Jesus' dying love
To bring you home to glory.

### 218

Broad is the road that leads to death,
And thousands walk together there;
But wisdom shows a narrow path,
With here and there a traveler.

2 "Deny thyself and take thy cross,"
Is the Redeemer's great command;
Nature must count her gold but dross,
If she would gain the heavenly land.

3 The fearful soul that tires and faints,
And walks the ways of God no more,
Shall be esteemed no more a saint,
And make his own destruction sure.

4 Lord! let not all my hopes be vain;
Create my heart entirely new,
Which hypocrites could ne'er attain,
Which false apostates never knew.

5 Sinner! perhaps this very day
Thy last accepted time may be;
Oh, shouldst thou grieve him now away,
Then hope may never beam on thee.

## No. 219.
## TIME SPEEDS AWAY.

Arranged by FANNIE BIRDSALL.

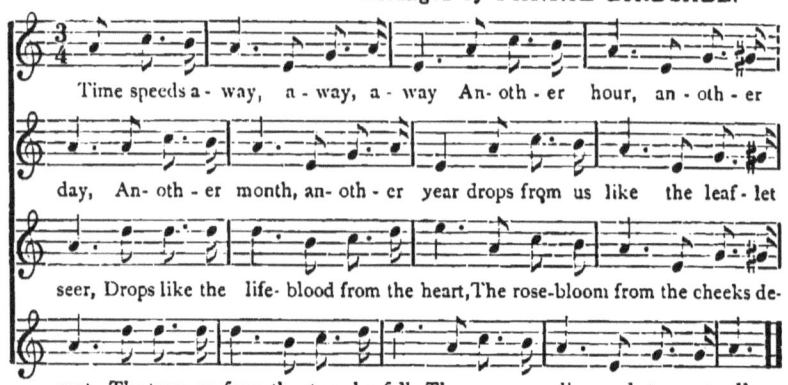

Time speeds a-way, a-way, a-way An-oth-er hour, an-oth-er day, An-oth-er month, an-oth-er year drops from us like the leaf-let seer, Drops like the life-blood from the heart, The rose-bloom from the cheeks de-part, The tress-es from the temples fall, The eyes grow dim and strange to all.

2 Time speeds away, away, away,
Like torrents in a stormy day;
He undermines the stately tower,
Uproots the tree, and blasts the flower;
He tears from our distracted breasts
The friends we loved, the friends that blest,
And leaves us weeping on the shore,
To which they can return no more.

3 Time speeds away, away, away,
No eagle through the sky of day;
No winds along the hills can flee
So swiftly or so smooth as he;
Like fiery steeds, from stage to stage,
He bears us on from youth to age;
Then plunges in the fearful sea
Of fathomless eternity.

4 Time speeds away, away, away,
O sinners, turn without delay
With rapid strides you onward go,
Down through the tomb, to endless woe.
Make haste! make haste! your time'll be past
In outer darkness you'll be cast;
Then what will be your dreadful state,
To hear pronounced, "Too late, too late!"

5 Time past away, away, away,
Forever gone, salvation's day,
Forever past your day of grace,
You must be banished from his face;
In outer darkness—there to dwell,
In keen despair,—an awful bell,
In blackest night of endless woe,
O do not to that darkness go.

## No. 220.

How lost was my condition,
Till Jesus made me whole,
There is one but Physician
Can cure a sin-sick soul.

CHO—There's a balm in Gilead,
To make the wounded whole,
There's power enough in Jesus
To cure a sin-sick soul.

2 Next door to death he found me,
And snatched me from the grave,
I tell to all around me
His wondrous power to save.

3 The worst of all diseases,
Is light compared with sin,
On every part it seizes,
But rages most within.

4 'Tis palsy, plague, and fever,
And madness, all combined,
And none but a believer,
The least relief can find.

5 From men great skill professing
I thought a cure to gain,
But this proved more distressing
And added to my pain.

6 Some said that nothing ailed me,
Some gave me up for lost!
Thus every refuge failed me,
And all my hopes were crossed.

7 At length, this great Physician—
How matchless is his grace!
Accepted my petition,
And undertook my case.

8 A dying, risen Jesus,
Seen by the eye of faith,
At once from danger frees us
And saves the soul from death.

9 Come, then, to this Physician,
His help he'll freely give,
He makes no hard condition,
'Tis only look and live.

## 221
## 'TIS THE LAST CALL OF MERCY.

Arranged by G. L. BROWN.

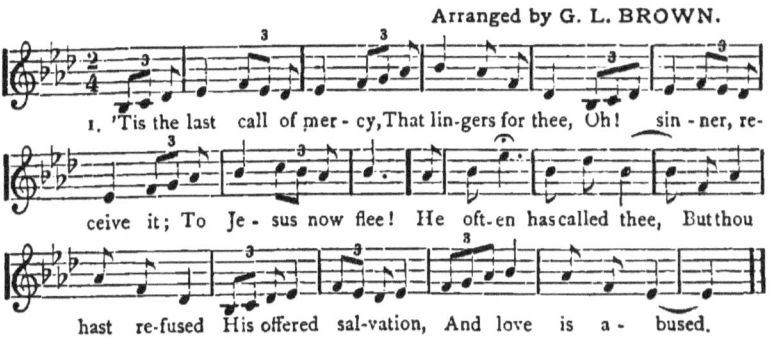

1. 'Tis the last call of mer-cy, That lin-gers for thee, Oh! sin-ner, re-ceive it; To Je-sus now flee! He oft-en has called thee, But thou hast re-fused His offered sal-vation, And love is a-bused.

2 If thou slightest this warning,
  Now offered at last,
  Thine will be the sad mourning
  "The harvest is past,
  Salvation I've slighted,
  The summer is o'er,
  And now there is pardon,
  Sweet pardon no more."

3 'Tis the last call of mercy,
  Oh, turn not away,
  For now swiftly hasteth
  The dread vengeance day!
  The Spirit invites you,
  And pleads with you, come!
  Oh, come to life's waters,
  Nor thirstingly roam!

4 'Tis the last call of mercy,
  Oh, steel not thy heart,
  For now she is rising,
  From earth to depart!
  The last note is sounding,
  The judgment is nigh!
  The Bridegroom is coming,
  Obey lest ye die.

5 'Tis the last call of mercy,
  That lingers for thee,
  Break away from thy bondage,
  O sinner, be free!
  Be not a sad mourner,
  "The harvest is past,
  The summer is ended,"
  And perish at last.

## 222
## A LITTLE MORE FAITH IN JESUS.

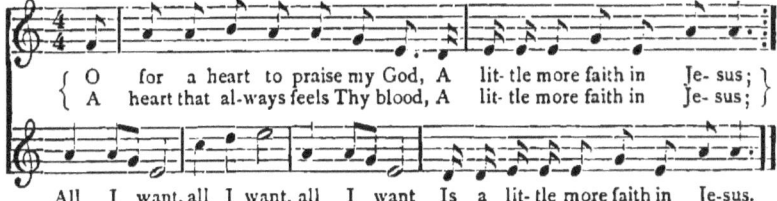

O for a heart to praise my God, A lit-tle more faith in Je-sus;
A heart that al-ways feels Thy blood, A lit-tle more faith in Je-sus;
All I want, all I want, all I want Is a lit-tle more faith in Je-sus.

2 A heart resign'd, submissive, meek,
  My great Redeemer's throne,
  Where only Christ is heard to speak,
  Where Jesus reigns alone.

3 Oh, for a lowly, contrite heart,
  Believing, true and clean!
  Which neither life nor death can part
  From Him that dwells within.

4 A heart in every thought renewed,
  And full of love divine;
  Perfect, and right, and pure, and good,
  A copy, Lord, of Thine.

5 Thy nature, gracious Lord impart;
  Come quickly from above;
  Write Thy new name upon my heart—
  Thy new, best name of Love.

# HIGHWAY HYMNAL.

## 223

I storm the gate of strife,
I force my passage through;
And all intent on endless life,
The narrow way pursue.

CHORUS.

I've taken the narrow way,
I've taken the narrow way,
With the sanctified few,
Who love to go through,
I've taken the narrow way.

2 I leave the world behind,
After my Lord to go,
Renouncing with a steadfast mind,
Its pride, and pomp of show.

3 My Father, he is God,
My heritage a throne;
And shall I herd with fashion's brood,
Or put her baubles on?

4 The tinselry of earth,
The trappings of its pride,
Unworthy of my heavenly birth,
I spurn them all aside.

5 No cumbrous garb I wear,
My progress to impede;
My pilgrim robe, divinely fair
Is fashioned for all speed.

6 I cannot slack my pace,
For earth's fantastic show;
For like a flint I've set my face
That I'll to Zion go.

7 Let fashion's maniac throng,
Hold senseless by her spell,
In idiot frenzy dance along,
And swarm the road to hell.

8 Ye gaudy fluttering crew,
In vain you smile or frown;
I cannot stop your toys to view;
I'm running for a crown!

9 I seem to tread in air,
I seem to walk with wings,
As toward my heavenly mansions fair
My soul exultant springs.

10 Right through this world of sin,
Its frantic cares and strife,
Its Babel war and dust and din;
I rush to endless life.

## 224

I have a never failing bank,
A more than golden store;
No earthly bank is half so rich—
How then can I be poor?

CHO—There's a plenty, a plenty, a plenty,
Oh! there's a plenty, in Zion's bank above.

2 'Tis when my stock is spent and gone,
And I without a groat,
I'm glad to hasten to my bank,
And beg a little note.

3 Sometimes my Banker, smiling says:
"Why don't you oft'ner come?
And when you draw a little note,
Why not a larger sum?

4 "Why live so meagrely and poor?
Your bank contains a plenty;
Why come and take a one-pound note,
When you might have a twenty?

5 "Yea, twenty thousand, ten times told,
Is but a trifling sum,
To what your Father has laid up,
Secure in God his Son."

6 Since then my Banker is so rich,
I have no cause to borrow;
I'll live upon my cash to-day,
And draw again to-morrow.

7 I've been a thousand times before,
And never was rejected;
Sometimes my Banker gives me more
Than asked for or expected.

8 Sometimes I've felt a little proud,
I've managed things so clever,
But ah! before the day was gone
I've felt as poor as ever.

9 I know my bank will never break—
No, it can never fail:
The firm—Three persons in one God;
Jehovah—Lord of all!

10 Should all the banks of Britain break,
The bank of England smash—
Bring in your notes to Zion's bank,
You'll surely have your cash.

11 And if you have but one small note,
Fear not to bring it in;
Come boldly to this bank of grace—
The Banker is within.

12 All forged notes will be refused,
Man's merits are rejected;
There's not a single note will pass,
That God has not accepted.

13 This bank is free to all the poor,
So plenteous is its store,
There's enough for each—enough for all,
And enough forevermore.

## 225

O, for a faith that will not shrink,
Though pressed by every foe,
That will not tremble on the brink
Of any earthly woe;

2 That will not murmur or complain
Beneath the chastening rod,
But, in the hour of grief or pain,
Will lean upon its God;

3 A faith that shines more bright and clear
When tempests rage without;
That when in danger knows no fear,
In darkness feels no doubt;

4 That bears unmoved, the world's dread frown,
Nor heeds its scornful smile;
That seas of trouble cannot drown,
Or satan's arts beguile;

5 A faith that keeps the narrow way,
Till life's last hour is fled,
And with a pure and heavenly ray
Illumes a dying bed.

# I Am With Thee Every Hour.

Arranged from a "Jubilee Song," by J. H. T.

1. I am with thee ev-ery hour, O ransomed one, For too
   I am with thee ev-ery hour, trust thou in Me, For My
2. I am with thee ev-ery hour, I know thy care, I will
   I am with thee ev-ery hour, My strength is thine, Thou the
3. I am with thee ev-ery hour, till life's work done, I shall
   I am with thee ev-ery hour, and Heav-en waits To throw

long the way, and dark, for thee a-lone:
love un-change-a-ble is pledged to thee.
cheer thy troub-led heart, thy bur-dens bear;
ten-der branch, and I the liv-ing vine.
bear thee hence to stand be-fore the throne:
o-pen wide for thee its pear-ly gates.

I am with thee, yes, I'm with thee, with thee, Ev-ery hour I'm with thee, with thee,

Thou art mine, for thee my life I gave!... I am with thee, yes, I'm with thee,

with thee, Ev-ery hour I'm with thee, with thee, With my love I'll guard, and guide, and save!

## No. 227
## Awake, O Heavenly wind.

THOMAS ROW.  
*Rather Slow.*  
THOS. B. CUNNINGHAM.

1. Awake, O heavenly wind, Thou Spirit most divine! Come blow upon thy garden here, And make its graces shine. Let ev-ery fruit-ful plant And fragrant spice be seen, To make the garden of our God Most pleasant and serene.

2. Come, sweet celestial Dove, In thy reviving gales, And tune our souls to sing the Lamb Whose kindness never fails; Let his sweet name perfume The garden of thy care; And fill our songs and every breath With thy delightful air.

*D.S. with the long expected shower, And fill the sacred place.*

CHORUS.

O Spirit most divine! In this accepted hour, As on the day of Pentecost, Descend in all thy pow'r; Come with thy promis'd help, Come with almighty grace, Come

ım;
ıin,

one.
part.
amb.
in.

ıw;

e,
e.

s.

## 233

Tune—"Life on the Ocean Wave."

'Tis better to shout than doubt,
'Tis better to shout than fall,
'Tis better to shout ten thousand times,
Than not to shout at all.
'Tis better to shout than weep,
'Tis better to shout than sin,
We do not want an empty shout,
'Tis better with glory in.

Cho—The glory makes me shout,
The glory makes me shout,
We march and sing and pray and believe,
'Till the glory makes us shout.

2 'Tis better to shout than doubt,
'Tis better to march than stand,
'Tis better to live to work and gain,
To die with a waving hand.
'Tis better to shout than fear,
'Tis better to work than rest,
Salvation shouts are rolling out,
God's glory shouts are best.

3 'Tis better to shout than doubt,
'Tis better to do and dare,
'Tis better to get the Lord to help
The Christians everywhere.
For the glory yet in store,
For the world is looking out,
'Tis better and better, more and more,
The glory makes me shout.

## 234

From "Penny Gospel Songs."

My Father is rich in houses and lands,
He holdeth the wealth of the world in his hands!
Of rubies and diamonds, of silver and gold;
His coffers are full, he has riches untold.

Chorus.

I'm the child of a King, the child of a King,
With Jesus my Saviour, I'm the child of a King.

2 My Father's own Son, the Saviour of men!
Once wandered o'er earth as the poorest of them!
But now He is reigning forever on high,
And will give us a home in the sweet by and by.

3 I once was an outcast, a stranger on earth,
A sinner by choice, and an "alien" by birth!
But I've been "adopted," my name's written down
An heir to a mansion, a robe and a crown.

4 A tent or a cottage, why should I care?
They're building a mansion for me over there,
Tho' exiled from home, yet still I may sing
All glory to God, I'm the child of a King.

## 235

From "Spiritual Songs."

The blood that flowed from Calvary,
From all my sins now cleanses me,
And I praise my Redeemer, my soul is free,
For the blood now cleanses me.

Cho—This fountain cleanses from all sin,
And every one may now plunge in;
There's a fountain, a fountain of water and blood,
Ever flowing for you and for me.

2 O, wonderful salvation this!
Unmeasured wealth of love and peace!
I will praise my Redeemer, my soul is free,
For the blood now cleanses me.

3 With joy I tell to others round
What depth of mercy I have found;
And I praise my Redeemer, my soul is free,
For the blood now cleanses me.

## 236

From "Holiness Songs," with per.

Tune—"Is not this the Land of Beulah?"

1 Sheltered in the Rock of Ages,
Kept from sin and all alarms,
The eternal God my refuge,
Safe in everlasting arms.
O how bulwarks pile around me;
Towers of strength and beauty shine,
Mighty fortress I have found thee,
Hid in God this soul of mine.

Chorus.

Though the storms may surge around me,
I can sing while billows roll,
For the mighty arms of Jesus
Clasp around my ransomed soul,

2 Blessed covert from the tempest,
Where secure my feet may stand;
Blessed Rock to give me shadow,
In a dry and weary land:
Tho' the foe may boast of shelter,
Yet their rock is not as ours;
Here the soul defies their legions,
Principalities and powers.

3 Covered in this Rock of Ages,
How the glory passes by,
Till like Moses on the mountain,
God is seen by mortal eye;
Changed from glory unto glory,
Safe from storm and tempest shock,
Here I rest secure forever,
In this blessed rifted Rock.

## 237

From "Holiness Songs," with per.

Tune—"Glory to His Name."

1 Precious salvation, so full and free,
Oh! that the world might Thy fulness see,
Jesus from sins and from sin sets free,
Jesus saves me now.

Chorus.

Jesus saves me now; Jesus saves me now,
Jesus from sin and from sins sets free,
Jesus saves me now.

2 Here at Thy feet I lay all my store,
Here is the life of my self will o'er,
All on the altar forevermore,
Jesus saves me now.

3 Now, Lord, I plunge 'neath the crimson tide,
Now I believe in the blood applied,
Now I believe I am sanctified,
Jesus saves me now.

4 Now is the body of sin destroyed,
Now I with Jesus am crucified,
Now to my soul is the blood applied,
Jesus saves me now.

5 Yes, from the traitor that lurked within,
From the desire and the bent to sin,
Jesus has saved me and keeps me clean,
Jesus saves me now.

## 238

From "Songs of Triumph," with per.

Hear the foot-steps of Jesus,
  He is now passing by,
Bearing balm for the wounded,
  Healing all who apply,
As he spake to the suff'rer
  Who lay at the pool,
He is saying this moment,
  "Wilt thou be made whole."

REFRAIN.

Wilt thou be made whole?
Wilt thou be made whole?
O come weary suff'rer, O come sin sick soul,
See, the life-stream is flowing,
See, the cleansing waves roll,
Step into the current and thou shalt be whole.

2 'Tis the voice of that Saviour,
  Whose merciful call
Freely offers salvation
  To one and to all;
He is now beck'ning to Him
  Each sin tainted soul,
And lovingly asking,
  "Wilt thou be made whole."

3 Are you halting and struggling,
  O'er-pow'red by your sin,
While the waters are troubled
  Can you not enter in?
Lo the Saviour stands waiting
  To strengthen your soul,
He is earnestly pleading,
  "Wilt thou be made whole."

4 Blessed Saviour assist us
  To rest on Thy word;
Let the soul-healing power
  On us now be out-poured;
Wash away ev'ry sin spot,
  Take perfect control,
Say to each trusting spirit,
  "Thy faith makes me whole."

## 239

From "Songs of Triumph," with per.

Thanks be to Jesus, His mercy is free,
Mercy is free, mercy is free,
Sinner that mercy is flowing for thee,
Mercy is boundless and free,
If thou art willing on Him to believe,
Mercy is free, mercy is free,
Life everlasting thy soul may receive,
Mercy is boundless and free.

REFRAIN.

Jesus my Saviour is looking for thee,
Looking for thee, looking for thee,
Lovingly, tenderly calling for thee
Calling and looking for thee.

2 Why on the mountains of sin wilt thou roam?
Gently the Spirit is calling, "Come home,"
Thou art in darkness, O come to the light,
Jesus is waiting, He'll save you to-night.

3 Think of His goodness, His patience and love,
Pleading thy cause with His Father above,
Come and repenting, O, give Him thy heart.
Grieve Him no longer but come as thou art,

4 Yes, there is pardon for all who believe,
Come and this moment a blessing receive,
Jesus is waiting, O, hear Him proclaim,
Cling to His mercy believe on his name.

## 240

From "Winnowed Hymns."

In God I have found a retreat,
  Where I can securely abide;
No refuge or rest so complete;
  And here I intend to reside.

CHO—O what comfort it brings,
  As my soul sweetly sings;
I am safe from all danger
  While under his wings.

2 I dread not the terror by night,
  No arrow can harm me by day,
His shadow has covered me quite,
  My fears he has driven away.

3 The pestilence walking about,
  When darkness has settled abroad,
Can never compel me to doubt
  The presence and power of God.

4 The wasting destruction at noon
  No fearful foreboding can bring;
With Jesus my soul doth consume,
  His perfect salvation I sing.

5 A thousand may fall at my side,
  And ten thousand at my right hand;
Above me his wings are spread wide,
  Beneath them in safety I stand.

## 241

From "Gems of Gospel Song," with per.

All my life long I had panted
  For a draught from some cool spring,
That I hoped would quench the burning,
  Of the thirst I felt within.

CHO—Hallelujah! I have found it.
  What my soul so long has craved!
Jesus satisfies my longing,
  Through his blood I now am saved,

2 Feeding on the husks around me,
  Till my strength was almost gone,
Longed my soul for something better,
  Only still to hunger on.

3 Poor I was, and sought for riches,
  Something that would satisfy,
But the dust I gathered round me
  Only mocked my soul's sad cry.

4 Well of water, ever springing,
  Bread of life so rich and free,
Untold wealth that never faileth,
  My Redeemer is to me.

## 242

"Gems of Gospel Song, with per."

Floods of mercy break around us,
  Jesus comes, comes to save!
Fetters fall that long have bound us,
  Jesus comes, comes to save!

CHO—Hallelujah! joyful story,
  Jesus comes, the King of glory!
Hallelujah! hallelujah!
  Jesus comes, comes to save.

2 While like rain our tears are falling, &c.
  While these souls for help are calling, &c.

3 Glorious light is dawning o'er us, &c.
  And the way grows bright before us, &c.

4 Hallelujah! saints are singing, &c.
  Heaven with joyous song is ringing, &c.

# HIGHWAY HYMNAL. 113

## 243

I know I love thee better, Lord,
Than any earthly joy,
For thou hast given me the peace
Which nothing can destroy.

Cho—The half has never been told,
Of love so full and free;
The half has never yet been told,
The blood—it cleanseth me.

2 I know that thou art nearer still
Than any earthly throng,
And sweeter is the thought of thee
Than any lovely song.

3 Thou hast put gladness in my heart;
Then well may I be glad!
Without the secret of thy love
I could not but be sad.

4 O, Saviour, precious Saviour mine!
What will thy presence be
If such a life of joy can crown
Our walk on earth with thee?
—Francis R. Havergal.

## 244

Wake, sinner, wake! there's no time for sleep;
Rouse from your slumber, there's danger on the deep!
Look to the Lord, for his grace to save and keep;
There is peace and safety only in the Life-Boat.

Chorus.

Come into the Life-Boat! Come into the Life-Boat!
Safely ride the angry foam;
Come into the Life-Boat! Come into the Life-Boat!
She will bring you safely home.

2 The storms they are heavy, the winds are loud,
The thunder is rolling and bursting in the cloud,
Fathers and mothers are crying so loud,
Jesus will take us in the Life-Boat.

3 Sinner, repent, and a new life begin;
Come to the Life-Boat, and quickly enter in;
Come, and be rescued from all your woe and sin,
There is peace and safety in the Life-Boat.

4 Praise the Redeemer! the work now is done;
Sin has been vanquish'd, the victory is won;
Go tell to others what Christ for you has done,
For he saved a dying sinner in the Life-Boat.

## 245

From "Blood Washed Songs."

Is there any sad heart that is heavy laden?
Any one here? Any one here?
Is there any poor soul who would love the Saviour?
Come and he will help you on your way.

Chorus.

Just as you are, the Lord will save you,
Come without delay;
Is there any poor soul who would follow Jesus?
Come and we will help you on your way.

2 Is there any who thirst for the living water? &c.
Is there any who sighs for the crimson fountain? &c.

3 Is there any who asks for a word of comfort? &c.
Is there any who feels that our prayr's would cheer you? &c.

4 Is there any who longs to be owned of Jesus? &c.
Is there any will say, I believe this moment? &c.

## 246

When the clouds are gathering round thee,
Look above and trust in God;
Be not weary of thy labor,
Tread the path thy Saviour trod.
Be not weary—
Toil, endure, and reap reward.

2 Take thy place among the workers,
In the fields of whitening grain
Take thy place and bear thy burden,
Thou shalt bear it not in vain,
Be not weary—
Thou a rich reward shall gain.

3 Call the many that surround thee,
All the needy, faint, unfed,
From the highways and the hedges,
To the Gospel Banquet spread.
Be not weary—
Break for them the living bread.

4 Faint not, fear not night's dark shadows,
One by one shall pass away;
Look! behold the dawn of morning,
Breaks with bright and cheering ray.
Be not weary—
God will bring the promised day.
—Selected

## 247

From "Spiritual Songs.

Lord, I care not for riches,
Neither silver nor gold,
I would make sure of heaven,
I would enter the fold.
In the book of thy kingdom,
With its pages so fair,
Tell me, Jesus, My Saviour,
Is my name written there?

Cho—Yes my name's written there
On the page white and fair;
In the book of Thy kingdom,
Yes my name's written there.

2 Lord, my sins they were many,
Like the sands of the sea,
But Thy blood, Oh, my Saviour!
Was sufficient for me;
For Thy promise is written
In bright letters that glow,
"Though your sins be as scarlet,
I will make them like snow."

3 Oh! that beautiful city,
With its mansions of light,
With its glorified beings,
In pure garments of white.
Where no evil thing cometh,
To despoil what is fair;
Where the angels are watching,
Is my name written there?

## 248
**CHILDREN'S PRAYERS.**

**NIGHT.**

"Now I lay me down to sleep,
I pray Thee, Lord, my soul to keep
If I should die before I wake
I pray Thee, Lord, my soul to take
And this I ask for Jesus sake."

**MORNING.**

Now 'tis morn and I'm awake,
My little prayer to thee I'll make,
I thank Thee, Lord, for thou hast kept
My soul and body while I slept,
Keep me to-day from sin and shame
And this I ask in Jesus' Name.
      GEO. L. BROWN.

---

## 249

1 There is a happy land,
 Far, far away,
 Where saints in glory stand,
 Bright, bright as day;
 Oh, how they sweetly sing,
 Worthy is our Saviour King,
 Loud let his praises ring,
 For evermore !

2 Come to that happy land;
 Come, come away;
 Why will ye doubting stand,
 Why still delay?
 Oh, we shall happy be,
 When, from sin and sorrow free;
 Lord, we shall live with thee,
 Blessed ever more.

3 Bright in that happy land,
 Beams every eye;
 Kept by a Father's hand;
 Love cannot die;
 Oh, then to glory run;
 Be a crown and kingdom won,
 And bright above the sun,
 Reign ever more.

## 250

1 Oh, do not be discouraged,
 For Jesus is your friend !
 Oh, do not be discouraged,
 For Jesus is your Friend !
 He will give you grace to conquer,
 He will give you grace to conquer,
 And keep you to the end.

**CHORUS.**

I am glad I'm in this army,
Yes, I'm glad I'm in this army,
Yes, I'm glad I'm in this army,
And I'll battle for the Lord.

2 Fight on, ye little soldiers,
 The battle you shall win;
 Fight on, ye little soldiers,
 The battle you shall win;
 For the Saviour is your Captain,
 For the Saviour is your Captain,
 And he has vanquished sin.

3 And when the conflict's over,
 Before him you shall stand;
 And when the conflict's over,
 Before him you shall stand,
 You shall sing his praise forever,
 You shall sing his praise forever,
 In Canaan's happy land.

## 251

1 I am so glad that our Father in heaven
 Tells of his love in the book he has given.
 Wonderful things in the Bible I see;
 This is the dearest that Jesus loves me.

**CHORUS.**

I am so glad that Jesus loves me,
Jesus loves me, Jesus loves me,
I am so glad that Jesus loves me,
Jesus loves even me,

2 Though I forget him and wander away,
 Still he doth love me wherever I stray;
 Back to his dear loving arms would I flee,
 When I remember that Jesus loves me.

3 In this assurance I find sweetest rest,
 Trusting in Jesus I know I am blest;
 Satan dismayed from my soul doth now flee,
 When I just tell him that Jesus loves me.

4 Jesus loves me and I know I love him,
 Love brought him down my poor soul to redeem
 Yes, it was love made him die on the tree,
 Oh ! I am certain that Jesus loves me.

5 If one should ask of me, how I can tell?
 Glory to Jesus! I know very well;
 God's Holy Spirit with mine doth agree
 Constantly witnessing—Jesus loves me .

6 Oh ! if there's only one song I can sing,
 When in his beauty I see the great King,
 This shall my song in eternity be,
 "Oh! what a wonder that Jesus loves me."

## 252

1 I gave my life for thee,
 My precious blood I shed,
 That thou might'st ransomed be,
 And quickened from the dead;
 I gave, I gave my life for thee,
 What hast thou given for Me?

2 My Father's home of light,—
 My glory-circled throne
 I left for earthly night,
 For wand'rings sad and lone,
 I left, I left it all for thee,
 Hast thou left aught for Me?

3 I suffered much for thee,
 More than thy tongue can tell,
 Of bitterest agony,
 To rescue thee from hell;
 I've borne, I've borne it all for thee,
 What hast thou borne for Me?

4 And I have brought to thee,
 Down from My home above,
 Salvation full and free,
 My pardon and My love;
 I bring, I bring rich gifts to thee,
 What hast thou brought to Me?

## 253

"Tis religion that can give
Sweetest pleasure while we live;
'Tis religion must supply
Solid comfort when we die.

CHO—Let us walk, &c.

2 After death its joys shall be
 Lasting as eternity;
 Be the living God our friend,
 Then our bliss shall never end.

## 254

From "Winnowed Hymns."

My hope is built on nothing less
Than Jesus' blood and righteousness;
I dare not trust the sweetest frame,
But wholly lean on Jesus' name.

Cho—On Christ, the Solid Rock, I stand;
‖All other ground is sinking sand.‖

2 When darkness seems to veil His face
I rest on his unchanging grace;
In every high and stormy gale,
My anchor holds within the vail.

3 His oath, His covenant, and blood,
Support me in the whelming flood:
When all around my soul gives way,
He then is all my hope and stay.

## 255

1 There is a spot to me more dear
Than native vale or mountain,
A spot for which affection's tear
Springs grateful from its fountain.
'Tis not where kindred souls abound,
Tho' that is almost heaven;
But where I first my Saviour found
And felt my sins forgiven!

2 Hard was my toil to reach the shore,
Long toss'd upon the ocean;
Above me was the thunder's roar,
Beneath, the waves' commotion;
Darkly the pall of night was thrown
Around me, faint with terror;
In that lone hour how did my groans
Ascend for years of error!

3 Fainting and panting, as for breath,
I knew not help was near me;
I cried, O save me, Lord, from death!
Immortal Jesus, save me!
Then, quick as tho't, I felt him mine;
My Saviour stood before me;
I saw his brightness round me shine,
And shouted Glory! Glory!

4 O happy hour! O hallow'd spot!
Where love divine first found me;
Wherever falls my distant lot,
My heart shall linger round thee:
And when from earth I rise and soar
Up to my home in heaven,
Down will I cast my eyes once more
Where I was first forgiven.

## 256

From the "Revivalist."

1 My latest sun is sinking fast,
My race is nearly run;
My strongest trials now are past,
My triumph is begun.

Chorus.

O come, angel band,
Come and around me stand,
‖: O, bear me away on your snowy wings
To my immortal home. :‖

2 I know I'm nearing the holy ranks
Of friends and kindred dear,
For I brush the dew on Jordan's banks
The crossing must be near,

3 I've almost gained my heavenly home.
My spirit loudly sings;

The holy ones, behold they come!
I hear the noise of wings.

4 O bear my longing heart to Him
Who bled and died for me;
Whose blood now cleanses from all sin,
And gives me victory.

## 257

To thee now, dear Christ, I'm clinging,
All my refuge and my plea;
Matchless is thy loving kindness,
Else it had not stoop'd to me.

Chorus.

Oh, 'tis glory! oh, 'tis glory!
Oh, 'tis glory in my soul!
For I've touched the hem of his garment,
And his pow'r doth make me whole.

2 Long my heart hath heard thee calling,
But I thrust aside thy grace;
Yet, O, boundless condescension,
Love is shining from thy face.

3 Love eternal, light eternal,
Close me safely, sweetly in;
Saviour, let thy balm of healing,
Ever keep me free from sin.

## 258

'Twas Jesus my Saviour who died on the tree,
To open a fountain for sinners like me,
His blood is that fountain which pardon bestows,
And cleanses the foulest wherever it flows.

Chorus.

‖For the Lion of Judah shall break ev'ry chain,
And give us the victory again and again.‖

2 When I was willing with all things to part,
He gave me my bounty, his love in my heart;
So now I am joined with the conquering band,
Who are marching to glory at Jesus' command.

3 And when with the ransomed, by Jesus my head,
From fountain to fountain I then shall be led,
I'll fall at his feet, and his mercy adore,
And sing of the blood of the cross evermore.

## 259

The holy war is raging,
And the foe is gathering round
To capture Zion's soldiers,
Or drive them from the ground.

Cho—Don't you know that Zion's soldiers
Stand firmly in the fight?
And the more you do oppose them
The stronger is their might.

2 The foe steps quick and sprightly,
Like a spirit is their tramp;
But the roar of Judah's Lion
Throws terror in their camp.

3 We see the shining armor
Of the soldiers in the field;
The holy courage on their brow
Seems to say they will not yield.

4 We read upon their banners
In words of living light,
That one can chase a thousand,
And two ten thousand flight.

## 260

1 Come believer, hung'ring, thirsting,
  Come a living sacrifice,
  God will sanctify you wholly,
  Cleanse and fit you for the skies.

CHO.—Come to the cross for full salvation
  Now the Comforter receive,
  Perfect peace, and full salvation
  God the Holy Ghost will give.

2 Now believer, come and welcome,
  God's free bounty glorify;
  Come in faith and consecration,
  All your fleshly hopes deny.

3 Lo! the Holy Ghost descending!
  Now behold the cleansing blood.
  Venture on Him, venture freely,
  Plunge beneath the crimson flood.

4 Christ the Comforter has promised
  To the pardoned child of God,
  Oh believer come and seek Him,
  Let your soul be His abode.

5 He will 'stablish, fix and keep you,
  Rooted, grounded in His love.
  Calm your wav'ring heart and seal it,
  Seal it for His courts above.

6 Into all His Truth He'll lead you,
  All things teach you as you go,
  In the dying hour be with you
  Death's dark river guide you thro.'
  GEO. L. BROWN.

## 261

1 I will sing you a song of that beautiful land,
  The far away home of the soul,
  Where no storms ever beat on the glittering strand,
  While the years of eternity roll.

2 O, that home of the soul, in my visions and dreams
  Its bright Jasper walls I can see,
  Till I fancy but thinly the veil intervenes,
  Between that fair city and me.

3 That unchangeable home is for you and for me,
  Where Jesus of Nazarath stands;
  The King of all kingdoms forever is he,
  And he holdeth our crowns in his hands.

4 O, how sweet it will be in that beautiful land,
  So free from all sorrow and pain!
  With songs on our lips, and with harps in our hands,
  To meet one another again.

## 262

1 I hear the Saviour say,
  Thy strength indeed is small,
  Child of weakness, watch and pray,
  Find in me thine all in all.

CHO—Jesus paid it all,
  All to him I owe.
  Sin had left a crimson stain:
  He washed it white as snow.

2 Lord, now indeed I find
  Thy pow'r, and thine alone,
  Can change this heart of mine
  And make it all thine own.

3 For nothing good have I
  Whereby thy grace to claim—
  I'll wash my garments white
  In the blood of Calv'ry's Lamb.

4 Then down beneath the cross
  I lay my sin sick soul,
  I'm counting all but dross
  Thy blood now makes me whole.

## 263

1 You may sing of the beauty of mountain and dale,
  Of the silvery streamlet and flowers of the vale;
  But the place most delightful the earth can afford,
  Is the place of devotion—the house of the Lord.

2 You may boast of the sweetness of days' early dawn,
  Of the sky's softening graces when day is just gone;
  But there's no other season or time can compare
  With the hour of devotion—the season of prayer.

3 You may value the frienship of youth and of age,
  And select for your comrades the noble and sage;
  But the friends that most cheer me on life's rugged road,
  Are the friends of my Master—the children of God.

4 You may talk of your prospects, of fame or of wealth,
  And the hopes that so flatter the favorites of health;
  But the hope of bright glory—of heavenly bliss!
  Take away every other, and give me but this.

5 Ever hail, blessed temple, abode of my Lord!
  I will turn to thee often, to hear from his word;
  I will walk to thy altar, with those that I love,
  And delight in the prospects revealed from above.

## 264

1 He leadeth me! oh! blessed thought;
  Oh! words with heav'nly comfort fraught;
  Whate'er I do, where'er I be,
  Still 'tis God's hand that leadeth me,

REF.—He leadeth me, He leadeth me!
  By his own hand he leadeth me;
  His faithful follower I would be,
  For by his hand he leadeth me.

2 Sometimes 'mid scenes of deepest gloom,
  Sometimes where Eden's bowers bloom,
  By waters still, o'er troubled sea,—
  Still 'tis his hand that leadeth me.

4 Lord, I would clasp thy hand in mine,
  Nor ever murmur nor repine—
  Content whatever lot I see,
  Since 'tis my God that leadeth me.

## 265

I love to tell the story
Of unseen things above,
Of Jesus and his glory,
Of Jesus and his love;
I love to tell the story,
Because I know it's true,
It satisfies my longings,
As nothing else would do.

Cho—I love to tell the story,
'Twill be my theme in glory
To tell the old, old story,
Of Jesus and his love.

2 I love to tell the story;
More wonderful it seems
Than all the golden fancies
Of all our golden dreams,
I love to the story;
It did so much for me!
And that is just the reason
I tell it now to thee.

4 I love to tell the story!
For those who know it best
Seem hungering and thirsting
To hear it like the rest.
And when, in scenes of glory,
I sing the NEW, NEW SONG,
'Twill be—the OLD, OLD STORY
That I have loved so long.

## 266

Holy Spirit, faithful Guide,
Ever near the Christian's side,
Gently lead us by the hand,
Pilgrims in a desert land,
Weary souls forc'er rejoice,
While they hear that sweetest voice,
Whisp'ring softly, wanderer, come!
Follow me, I'll guide thee home.

2 Ever present, truest friend,
Ever near, thine aid to lend;
Leave us not to doubt and fear,
Groping on in darkness drear.
When the storms are raging sore,
Hearts grow faint and hopes give o'er,
Whisper sofly, wanderer, come!
Follow me, I'll guide thee home.

3 When our days of toil shall cease,
Waiting still for sweet release,
Nothing left but heaven and prayer,
Knowing that our names are there;
Wading deep the dismal flood,
Pleading naught but Jesus' blood;
Whisper softly, wanderer, come!
Follow me, I'll guide thee home.

## 267

Jesus, my all to heaven is gone,
He, whom I fix my hopes upon;
His track I see, and I'll pursue
The narrow way till him I view.
The way the holy prophets went—
The road that leads from banishment,—
The King's highway of holiness,
I'll go, for all his paths are peace.

2 This is the way I long have sought,
And mourned because I found it not;
My grief a burden long has been,
Because I was not saved from sin.
The more I strove against its power,
I felt its weight and guilt the more;
Till late I heard my Saviour say,
Come hither, soul, I am the way.

3 Lo! glad I come; and thou, blest Lamb,
Shalt take me to thee as I am;
Nothing but sin have I to give—
Nothing but love shall I receive.
Then will I tell to sinners round
What a dear Saviour I have found;
I'll point to thy redeeming blood,
And say, Behold the way to God.

## 268

How happy is the man who has chosen wisdom's ways,
And measured out his span to his God in pray'r and praise;
His God and his Bible are all that he desires,
To holiness of heart he continually aspires;
In poverty he's happy, for he knows he has a friend
Who never will forsake him till the world shall have an end.

2 He rises in the morning, with the lark he tunes his lays,
And offers up a tribute to his God in prayer and praise,
And then to his labor he cheerfully repairs,
In confidence believing that God will hear his prayers.
Whatever he engages in at home or abroad,
His object is to honor and to glorify his God.

3 In sickness, pain and sorrow, he never will repine,
While he is drawing nourishment from Christ the living vine;
When trouble presses heavily he leans on Jesus' breast,
And in his precious promises he finds a quiet rest;
The yoke of Christ is easy, and his burden always light,
He lives, nor is he weary till Canaan heaves in sight.

4 'Tis thus you have his history thro' life from day to day,
Religion is no mystery, with him 'tis a beaten way;
And when upon his pillow he lies down to die,
In hope he rejoices for he knows his God is nigh;
And when life's lamp is flickering, his soul on wings of love
Away to realms of glory flies to reign with Christ above.

## 269

The day is past and gone,
The evening shades appear;
Oh, may we all remember well,
The night of death draws near.

2 We lay our garments by,
Upon our beds to rest;
So death will soon disrobe us all
Of what we here possess.

3 Lord, keep us safe this night,
Secure from all our fears;
May angels guard us while we sleep,
Till morning light appears.

4 And when we early rise,
And view th' unwearied sun,
May we set out to win the prize,
And after glory run.

5 And when our days are past,
And we from time remove,
Oh, may we in thy bosom rest,
The bosom of thy love.

## 270

There is an hour of peaceful rest
 To mourning wand'rers given;
There is a joy for souls distressed,
 A balm for every wounded breast—
'T is found above, in heaven.

2 There is a soft, a downy bed,
 'Tis fair as breath of even;
A couch for weary mortals spread,
Where they may rest the aching head,
 And find repose—in heaven.

3 There is a home for weary souls,
 By sin and sorrow driven;
When tossed on life's tempestuous shoals,
Where storms arise, and ocean rolls,
 And all is drear but heaven.

4 There faith lifts up her cheerful eye,
 To brighter prospects given;
And views the tempest passing by,
The evening shadows quickly fly,
 And all serene—in heaven.

5 There fragrant flowers immortal bloom
 And joys supreme are given;
There rays divine disperse the gloom,
Beyond the confines of the tomb
 Appears the dawn of heaven.

## 271

Sweet hour of prayer, sweet hour of prayer,
That calls me from a world of care,
And bids me at my Father's throne
Make all my wants and wishes known!
In seasons of distress and grief
My soul has often found relief,
And oft escaped the tempter's snare,
By thy return, sweet hour of prayer.

2 Sweet hour of prayer, sweet hour of prayer,
Thy wings shall my petition bear
To him, whose truth and faithfulness,
Engage the waiting soul to bless;
And since he bids me seek his face,
Believe his word and trust his grace,
I'll cast on him my every care,
And wait for thee, sweet hour of prayer.

## 272

In the cross of Christ I glory,
 Towering o'er the wrecks of time;
All the light of sacred story
 Gathers round its head sublime.

2 When the woes of life o'ertake me,
 Hopes deceive and fears annoy,
Never shall the Cross forsake me;
 Lo! it glows with peace and joy,

3 When the sun of bliss is beaming
 Light and love upon my way,
From the Cross the radiance streaming,
 Adds new luster to the day.

4 Bane and blessing, pain and pleasure,
 By the cross are sanctified;
Peace is there, that knows no measure,
 Joys that through all time abide.

## 273

Loving Saviour, hear my cry, hear my cry,
 hear my cry,
Trembling to Thine arms I fly,
 O, save me at the cross;
I have sinned, but Thou hast died, Thou hast
 died, Thou hast died,
In Thy mercy let me hide,
 O, save me at the cross.

Cho—Dear Jesus recieve me
 No more would I grieve Thee,
 Now blessed Redeemer,
 O, save me at the cross.

2 Though I perish, ‖I will pray,‖
Thou of life the living way.
 O, save me at the cross,
Thou hast said Thy ‖grace is free,‖
Have compassion, Lord on me,
 O, save me at cross.

3 Wash me in Thy ‖cleansing blood,‖
Plunge me now beneath that flood,
 O, save me at the cross.
Only faith will ‖pardon bring,‖
By that faith to Thee I cling,
 O, save me at the cross.

## 274

My heavenly home is bright and fair;
Nor pain, nor death can enter there;
Its glittering towers the sun outshine;
That heavenly mansion shall be mine.

Cho—We're going home, to die no more, &c.

2 My Father's house is built on high,
 Far, far above the starry sky.
When from this earthly prison free,
 That heavenly mansion mine shall be.

3 Let others seek a home below
 Which flames devour, or waves o'erflow;
Be thine the happier lot to own
 A heavenly mansion near the throne.

## 275

My days are gliding swiftly by,
 And I, a pilgrim stranger,
Would not detain them as they fly,
 These hours of toil and danger.

Cho—For now we stand on Jordan's strand,
 Our friends are passing over;
And just before the shining shore
 We may almost discover.

2 We'll gird our loins, my brethren dear,
 Our heavenly homes discerning;
Our absent Lord has left us word,
 Let every lamp be burning.

3 Let sorrow's rudest tempest blow,
 Each cord on earth to sever,
Our King says come, and there's our home,
 Forever, Oh, forever!

## 276

Come to Jesus, come to Jesus,
Come to Jesus just now,
Just now come to Jesus,
Come to Jesus just now.

He will save you, etc.
He is able, etc.
He is willing, etc.
He is waiting, etc.
He will hear you, etc.
He will cleanse you, etc.
He'll renew you, etc.
He'll forgive you, etc.
If you trust him, etc.
He will save you, etc.

## 277

To-day, if you will hear his voice,
Now is the time to make your choice,
Say, will you to mount Zion go?
Say, will you have this Christ or no?
Will you be saved from guilt and pain?
Will you with Christ for ever reign?
Say, will you be forever blest,
Will you with Christ forever rest?

Cho.—We are passing away
We are passing away
We are passing away
To the great judgment day.

2 Ye blooming youth, for ruin bound,
Obey the Gospel's joyful sound;
Come, go with us, and you shall prove
The joys of Christ's redeeming love.
Behold he's waiting at your door!
Make now your choice—Oh, halt no more,
Say, sinner, say, what will you do?
say, will you have this Christ or no?

3 Your sports, and all your glittering toys,
Compared to your celestial joys,
Like momentary dreams appear;
Come, go with us—your souls are dear.
Why rush in carnal pleasures on?
Why madly plunge in sorrow down?
Say, will you to mount Zion go?
Say, will you have this Christ or no?

4 Oh, must we bid you all farewell?
We bound to heaven, and you to hell!
Still God may hear us while we pray,
And change you, ere that burning day,
Once more we ask you in his name—
For yet his love remains the same?
Say, will you to mount Zion go?
Say, will you have this Christ or no?

## 278

Will you come, will you come, with your poor broken heart,
Burden'd and sin oppressed?
Lay it down at the feet of your Saviour and Lord.
Jesus will give you rest.

CHORUS.

O happy rest, sweet happy rest!
Jesus will give you rest,
Oh! why wont you come in simple trusting faith,
Jesus will give you rest.

2 Will you come, will you come? there is mercy for you,
Balm for your aching breast,
Only come as you are, and believe on his name,
Jesus will give you rest.

3 Will you come, will you come? you have nothing to pay,
Jesus who loves you best;
By his death on the Cross purchased life for your soul.
Jesus will give you rest.

4 Will you come, will you come? how he pleads with you now!
Fly to his loving breast;
And whatever your sin or your sorrow may be
Jesus will give you rest.

## 279

Come, every soul by sin oppressed,
There's mercy with the Lord,
And he will surely give you rest,
By trusting in his word.

Cho—Only trust him, only trust him,
Only trust him now;
He will save you, he will save you,
He will save you now.

2 For Jesus shed his precious blood
Rich blessings to bestow;
Plunge now into the crimson tide
That washes white as snow.

3 Yes Jesus is the Truth, the Way,
That leads you into rest;
Believe in him without delay,
And you are fully blest.

4 Come then and join this holy band
And on to glory go
To dwell in that celestial land
Where joys immortal flow.

## 280

Rock of Ages, cleft for me,
Let me hide my self in thee,
Let the water and the blood,
From thy wounded side which flowed,
Be of sin the double cure,
Save from wrath and make me pure.

2 Could my tears forever flow,
Could my zeal no languor know,
These for sin could not atone,
Thou must save, and thou alone;
In my hand no price I bring,
Simply to thy cross I cling.

3 While I draw this fleeting breath,
When my eyes shall close in death,
When I rise to worlds unknown,
And behold thee on the throne,
Rock of Ages, cleft for me,
Let me hide myself in thee.

## 281

Urge on your rapid course,
Ye blood-besprinkled bands;
The heavenly kingdom suffers force;
'Tis seized by violent hands.

CHORUS.

We'll drive this battle on;
We'll drive this battle on;
In Jesus' might, we'll stand and fight,
And drive this battle on.

2 Through much distress and pain,
Through many a conflict here,
Through blood, ye must the entrance gain;
Yet, oh, disdain to fear!

3 "Courage!" your Captain cries,
Who all your toil foreknew;
"Toil ye shall have, yet all despise;
I have o'ercome for you."

4 This is the victory,—
Before our faith they fall:
Jesus hath died for you and me;
Believe, and conquer all.

## 282

Copyright by T. B. Arnold, with per.

Awaken, ye people, and hear our glad song,
That bursts from our souls as we're marching
   along
A chorus of fire God sends thro' the land,
And we've come to sing it, the Holiness Band.

2 The upper room fire has ne'er lost its power,
The Comforter comes, as our helper each hour,
In this dispensation most glorious most grand,
We live and we labor, the Holiness Band.

3 We come with glad tidings, deliverance from
   sin,
His name was called Jesus this vict'ry to win,
No more need you struggle in sins sinking
   sand,
But come now and join us, the Holiness Band.

4 Our motto is Holiness unto the Lord,
O'er the world we will spread it, obeying his
   word,
His blood the heart washes and makes pure
   the hand,
From all sin he cleanseth the Holiness Band.

5 We've left all for Jesus, e'en life is at stake,
And no reservation of aught do we make;
We've counted the cost and through him we
   stand,
A hundred fold waits for the Holiness Band.

6 With Christ our commander, we know no
   defeat,
We've sounded a trumpet that ne'er calls re-
   treat,
Then onward, right onward, at his blest com-
   mand,
Clear the way, we are coming, the Holiness
   Band.

7 In the name of the Lord our banners we
   wave,
We trust not in horses or chariots to save,
In the strength of Jehovah, sin's hosts we
   withstand,
O think not we fear, we're the Holiness Band.

8 Let come fiery trials, and mockings, and
   hate,
And devil's howl round us to heaven's own
   gate;
No earth will can move us, what God doth de-
   mand
We hasten to do, sings the Holiness Band.

9 But soon all our labors on earth will be o'er
We'll suffer, we'll sorrow, we'll weep never-
   more;
We'll join all the blood-washed on heaven's
   bright strand,
For the saints all belong to the Holiness
   Band.

## 283

Fly to the arms of the Saviour,
  The arms that are open to thee;
O bathe in the fountain of mercy,
  The fountain so rich and so free.

Cho—O, turn to the light that is shining,
  Is shining so bright and so clear;
O, list to the voice that is speaking,
  Is speaking in accents so dear.

2 O, seek for the hope of the christian,
  The hope that will never betray;
O, ever be faithful to duty
  And angels will guard all thy way.

3 O, aim to inhabit the city,
  The city of crystal and gold;
O, strive to inherit the treasure,
  The treasure whose wealth is untold.

4 O seek for the crown that is promised,
  The crown which the conqueror's win;
The robe and the harp that are given,
  To those that shall enter therein.

                     Rev. E. H. Hall.

## 284

Jesus, I my cross have taken,
  All to leave and follow thee;
Naked, poor, despised, forsaken,
  Thou from hence my all shalt be,
Perish every fond ambition,
  All I've sought or hoped or known,
Yet how rich is my condition—
  God and heaven are still my own.

2 Let the world despise and leave me,
  They have left my Saviour too;
Human hearts and looks deceive me,
  Thou art not, like them, untrue.
And while thou shalt smile upon me,
  God of wisdom, love and might,
Foes may hate, and friends disown me
  Show thy face and all is bright.

3 Go, then, earthly fame and treasure;
  Come disaster, scorn, and pain;
In thy service pain is pleasure—
  With thy favor, loss is gain.
I have called thee Abba, Father,
  I have set my heart on thee;
Storms may howl, and clouds may gath-
   er,
  All must work for good to me.

4 Soul—then know thy full salvation,
  Rise o'er sin, and fear, and care,
Joy to fi'd, in every station.
  Something still to do or bear;
Think what spirit dwells within thee,
  Think what Father's smiles are thine;
Think that Jesus died to save thee;
  Child of heaven, canst thou repine?

5 Man may trouble and distress me,
  'T will but drive me to thy breast;
Life with trials hard may press me,
  Heaven will bring me sweeter rest
Oh! 'tis not in grief to harm me,
  While thy love is left to me;
Oh! 'twere not in joy to charm me,
  Were that joy unmixed with thee.

6 Haste thee on from grace to glory,
  Armed by faith, and winged by pray'r,
Heaven's eternal days before thee,
  God's own hand shall guide thee there
Soon shall close thine earthly mission,
  Soon shall pass thy pilgrim days
Hope shall change to glad fruition,
  Faith to sight, and prayer to praise.

## 285

O do not suffer aught to part
  The souls that here agree;
But make us of one mind and heart,
  And keep us one in thee.

2 Together let us sweetly live,
  Together let us die;
And each a starry crown receive,
  And reign above the sky.

## HIGHWAY HYMNAL.  121

### 286

One more day's work for Jesus;
One less of life for me!
But heav'n is nearer,
And Christ is dearer,
Than yesterday to me;
His love and light
Fill all my soul to-night.

Cho.—One more day's work for Jesus,
One more day's work for Jesus,
One more day's work for Jesus,
One less of life for me.

2 One more day's work for Jesus;
How glorious is my King!
'Tis joy, not duty,
To speak His beauty;
My soul mounts on the wing
At the mere thought
How Christ my life has bought.

3 One more day's work for Jesus;
How sweet the work has been.
To tell the story,
To show the glory,
When Christ's flock enter in!
How it did shine
In this poor heart of mine.

4 One more day's work for Jesus—
Oh yes, a weary day;
But heaven shines clearer,
And rest comes nearer,
At each step of the way;
And Christ in all—
Before His face I fall.

5 Oh, blessed work for Jesus!
Oh, rest at Jesus' feet!
There toil seems pleasure.
My wants are treasure,
And pain for Him is sweet.
Lord, if I may,
I'll serve another day.

### 287

From "Holiness Songs," with per.
Tune—"Have you been to Jesus for the cleansing power."

There's a fountain flowing from the Saviour's side,
That can sweep all the sin from thy soul.
There's a virtue dwelling in this crimson tide,
Makes the wounded ones perfectly whole.

Chorus.

Blessed fount, precious fount,
Where my Saviour has saved me from sin,
How my soul rejoices in the cleansing power,
And the fountain is keeping me clean.

2 To the house of David and Jerusalem,
Opened wide is this fountain to-day,
And His cleansing power can reach the least of them,
And can take all the sin curse away.

3 Thro' the Holy Spirit's sanctifying power,
Thro' the blood of the lamb that was slain,
Thro' the word of the promise I am saved this hour,
And the fountain has cleansed every stain.

4 I am in the fountain, and by faith I'll stay,
For its virtue is keeping me white;
And His perfect love has cast my fears away,
I am cleansed as I walk in the light.

### 288
Tune—No. 172.

How firm a foundation, ye saints of the Lord,
Is laid for your faith in his excellent word;
What more can he say, than to you he hath said,
To you, who for refuge to Jesus have fled?

2 In every condition, in sickness and health,
In poverty's vale, or abounding in wealth,
At home and abroad, on the land on the sea,
As thy days may demand, shall thy strength ever be.

3 Fear not, I am with thee—Oh! be not dismayed,
For I am thy God, and will still give thee aid;
I'll strengthen thee, help thee, and cause thee to stand
Upheld by my righteous, omnipotent hand.

4 When through the deep waters I call thee to go,
The rivers of woe shall not thee overflow;
For I will be with thee, thy troubles to bless,
And sanctify to thee thy deepest distress.

5 When through fiery trials thy pathway shall lie,
My grace all-sufficient shall be thy supply;
The flame shall not hurt thee, I only design
Thy dross to consume, and thy gold to refine.

6 E'en down to old age, all my people shall prove
My sovereign, eternal. unchangeable love;
And when hoary hairs shall their temples adorn,
Like lambs they shall still in thy bosom be borne.

7 The soul that on Jesus doth lean for repose,
I will not, I will not desert to his foes;
That soul, though all hell should endeavor to shake,
I'll never, no never, no never forsake.

### 289
First part of this hymn No. 156.

3 But there is a spot—one beautiful spot
My heart lingers o'er with emotion;
Its peaceful enjoyments shall ne'er be forgot;
'Tis the place of my former devotion.
I see it, "outstretched, in its loveliness," lie,
Like a garden of lilies and roses;
More charming to me, as it fades from the eye,
Than the valleys of Canaan, to Moses.'"

4 Lo! upward I gaze, and the glory supreme,
That illumines the heights of elysian,
Shines down through the veil—there is life in each beam—
It renders immortal my vision;
The notes of soft melody fall on my ear:
Harmonious the cadence and measure:
'Tis the voice of the harpers on Zion I hear;
Full high swells their chorus of pleasure.

5 Lo! there are the towers of my future abode,
The city on high and eternal!
See, there is the Eden—the river of God!
And the trees ever bearing and vernal:
Haste, haste with me onward, companion and guide,
Let me join in that heavenly matin;
Fly wide, ye bright gates! swiftly through them I ride,
Triumphant o'er sin, death, and Satan.

## Highway Hymnal.

### 290
*Altar Calls with Hymns to Suit.*
(Turn to this page and you will never lack
for an Invitation Hymn.)
Come ye sinners poor, &c., No. 28.
Come believer hung'ring, &c., No. 260.
O thou God of my salvation, &c., 96.
Come Thou Fount of every blessing, No. 5.
 Cho.—Turn to the Lord and seek salvation,
  Sound the praise of His dear Name,
  Glory, honor and salvation,
  Christ, the Lord has come to reign.
Also,
 Come to the cross for full salvation,
 Now the Comforter receive;
 Perfect peace and full salvation
 God the Holy Ghost will give.
Also,
 "The fountain lies open,"
 Sinner come and bathe your weary soul.
Also,
 "Why don't you come to Jesus,"
 Why don't you come to Jesus and be &c.
Also,
 I will arise and go to Jesus,
 He will embrace me in His arms;
 In the arms of my dear Saviour,
 O there are ten thousand charms.
Also,
 He is able, He is able,
 He is willing, doubt no more.

There is a fountain filled with blood, No. 21.
Come every soul by sin oppressed, &c., No. 279.
Am I a soldier of the cross, &c., No. 37.
Alas and did my Saviour bleed, &c., No. 189.
Forever here my rest shall be, &c., No. 142.
When I can read my title clear, &c., No. 229.
 Cho.—Come to Jesus, come to Jesus,
  Come to Jesus now;
  He will save you, He will save you,
  He will save you now.
Also,
 Only trust him, &c.
Also,
 There is power in Jesus' blood,
 There is power in Jesus' blood,
 There is power in Jesus' blood,
 To wash me white as snow.
  Or,
 To sanctify my soul,
Also,
 ":We will stand the storm
 We will anchor by and by.:"

Come to Jesus, &c., No. 276.
To-day if you will hear his voice, &c. No. 277.
Will you come, will you come, &c., No. 278.
Have you been to Jesus, &c. No. 75.
Jesus will help if you try, &c. No. 231.
I hear thy welcome voice, &c. No. 93.
O turn ye, O turn ye, &c., No. 150.
The Shepherd is tenderly calling, &c. No. 80.

### 291
*Faith or Consecration Hymns and
Choruses.*
(To be sung at the altar—softly while kneeling, triumphantly when rising.)
I am coming to the cross, &c., No. 92.
Jesus lover of my soul, &c., No. 171.
 Cho.—I am trusting Lord in thee,
  Dear Lamb of Calvary.
  Humbly at the cross I bow,
  Jesus saves me, saves me now.

Jesus, my Lord, to Thee I cry, &c., No. 26.
Just as I am without one plea, &c., No. 207.
 Cho.—"Take me as I am,"
  O bring thy free salvation nigh
  And take me as I am,
   Or,
  He takes me as I am.

While we bow in thy name, &c., No. 103.
O how happy are they, &c., No. 104.
 Cho.—"It is good to be here,"
  Thy perfect love now drives away all
    our fear;
  And the light streaming down,
  Makes our pathway all clear—
  It is good for us Lord, to be here.

There is a fount. &c. (See Altar Calls.)
 Cho.—"I'm believing,"
  I'm believing now on the Lord,
  "I'm receiving"
  Salvation through His word.
Also,
 I will believe, I do believe,
 That Jesus died for me;
 And through this blood, His precious blood,
 I am from sin set free.
Also,
 We will rest in the fair and happy land,
 Just across on the evergreen shore;
 Sing the song of Moses and the Lamb,
  by and by,
 And dwell with Jesus evermore.
Also,
 O glorious fountain, Here will I stay;
 And in Thee ever Wash my sins away.
Also,
 I am redeemed, I am redeemed,
 I'm washed in the blood of the
    Lamb
 Who died on Calvary.

A charge to keep I have, &c., No. 83.
And can I yet delay, &c., No. 100.
I hear thy welcome voice, &c., No. 93.
I storm the gate of strife, &c., No. 223.
 Cho.—Let us kneel 'round the altar
  Kneel round the altar
  Let us kneel round the altar
  And God will answer prayer.
Also,
 "I've taken the narrow way"
 With the resolute few
 Who dare to go through
 I've taken the narrow way.
Or, With the sanctified few, who love, &c.
Also, We'll drive this battle on, &c.

Also, I'm glad salvation's free, &c.
Also, There'll be no sorrow there, &c,
Also, There'll be no parting there, &c.
Also,
  I yield, I yield, I yield,
  I can hold out no more.

I know that my Redeemer lives, &c., No. 295
Cho—I can, and I will, and I do believe,
  That Jesus saves me now.

O God my heart doth long for thee, &c., No. 88.
Out on the promise, &c., No. 20.
O precious is the flow, &c., No. 66.
+ Take my poor heart, &c., No. 139.
'Tis done the great transaction's, &c., No. 125.
O now I see the crimson wave, No. 61.
I'm saved! I'm saved, &c., No. 247.
Lord in the strength of grace, No. 127.

## TABLE HYMNS.

### 292

To God we hymn our grateful praise,
For blessings new, that crown our days.
'Tis from Thy hand of love Divine,
We feed once more these bodies thine.

2 We thank Thee, Lord, for this our food,
But praise Thee more for Jesus' blood.
We eat and live to God alone,
Who makes our heart His blissful throne.

Be present at our table Lord,
Be here, as everywhere adored;
These comforts bless and grant that we
May feast in Paradise with Thee.

  Guide me, O Thou great Jehovah!
  Pilgrim to the heav'nly land;
  I am weak, but Thou art mighty;
  Hold me with thy powerful hand:
  Bread of heaven!
  Feed me till I want no more.

  In this earthly wilderness
  Thou hast a table spread,
  Richly filled with every grace,
  Our fainting souls can need:
  Still sustain us by thy love,
  Still thy servant's strength repair.
  Till we reach the courts above
  And feast forever there.

### 293

Prayer for a christian in sickness.

Our gracious Saviour and our Lord,
Who didst in days of yore,
By speaking but one healing word,
Another's servant cure—
Lo! here thy servant lieth ill,
For whom thy children care;
Thou art the Good Physician still—
Wilt thou not hear our prayer?

2 The same thou art in power and grace,
We cannot doubt thy love;
Though now in heaven before thy face
Ten thousand angels move:
With wrestling faith our hearts we pour
Before thy gracious throne,
Wouldst thou another's servant cure,
And not regard thine own?

3 Thine own thou surely dost regard,
Redeemed with precious blood,
And fit him for his high reward,
And chasten for his good:
Thy joyous love his heart sustain,
Thy grace his strength renew;
And quickly raise him up again,
His Master's work to do.

4 A single Roman soldier sent
His message, full of faith;
And thou, on works of mercy bent
His servant saved from death;
Behold they come, themselves, to thee,
Thine own disciples dear,
And bend in faith the suppliant knee,
And shed th' imploring tear.

5 Master Supreme, disease and woe
Thy sovereign voice obey;
At thy command they come and go,
Submissive to thy sway.
The word of healing mercy send
And in this self-same hour,
Oh, let thy servant, Lord, amend,
And glorify the power.

### 294
Faith-Cure Hymn.

My Father's Son, Jesus, who died on a tree,
Bought pardon and cleansing and healing, all three.
My body's redeemed, I can joyfully sing;
I'm free from disease, I'm a child of the King.

2 I once was a sufferer from pain and disease,
Through earthly physicians, I long sought release;
When, lo, Jesus said, "with my blood on the tree
I purchased thy healing, from sickness be free."

3 O, suffering believer, is faith's vision dim,
Thy sickness Christ bore, turn thine eyes unto him;
He bids thee be whole, then exultingly sing,
Redemption is purchased, I'm a child of the King.   Mrs. S. G. C.

### 295

  I know that my Redeemer lives,
   To intercede for me.

  I can, I will and I do believe,
  I can, I will and I do believe,
  I can, I will and I do believe,
  That Jesus saves me now.

  He wills that I should holy be,
   And dwell with Him above,

  He gave His life to set me free,
   And fit me for the skies.

  Here Lord I give myself away,
   'Tis all that I can do.

  The blood of Christ now cleanses me,
   As soon as I believe.

## 296

The great Physician now is near,
The sympathizing Jesus;
He speaks the drooping heart to cheer
Oh hear the voice of Jesus.

Cho—Sweetest note in seraph song,
Sweetest name on mortal tongue,
Sweetest carol ever sung,
Jesus, blessed Jesus.

2 Your many sins are all forgiven,
Oh, hear the voice of Jesus;
Go on your way in peace to heaven,
And wear a crown with Jesus.

3 All glory to the dying Lamb!
I now believe in Jesus;
I love the blessed Saviour's name,
I love the name of Jesus.

4 The children too, both great and small,
Who love the name of Jesus,
May now accept the gracious call
To work and live for Jesus.

5 Come, brethren, help me sing His praise,
Oh, praise the name of Jesus;
Come, sisters, all your voices raise,
Oh, bless the name of Jesus.

6 His name dispels my guilt and fear,
No other name but Jesus:
Oh, how my soul delights to hear
The precious name of Jesus.

7 And when to that bright world above,
We rise to see our Jesus,
We'll sing around the throne of love
His name, the name of Jesus.

## 297

"Songs of Triumph," with per.

Will your anchor hold in the storms of life,
When the clouds unfold their wings of strife;
When the strong tides lift and the cables strain,
Will your anchor drift, or firm remain?

Cho—We have an anchor that keeps the soul,
Steadfast and sure while the billows roll,
Fastened to the Rock which cannot move,
Grounded firm and deep in the Saviour's love.

2
It is safely moored, 'twill the storm withstand,
For 'tis well secured by the Saviour's hand;
And the cable's passed from his heart to mine,
Can defy the blast, through strength divine.

3
It will firmly hold in the straits of fear,
When the breakers have told the reef is near,
Though the tempest rave and the wild winds blow,
Not an angry wave shall our bark o'erflow.

4
It will surely hold in the floods of death,
When the waters cold chill our latest breath,
On the rising tide it can never fail,
While our hopes abide within the veil.

5
When our eyes behold through the gath'ring night,
The city of gold, our harbor bright,
We shall anchor fast by the heav'nly shore,
With the storms all past forevermore.

## 298

From "Holiness Songs," with per.

Tune—"I am Trusting, Lord, in Thee."

Jesus, Thou hast bid me live,
All my living powers I give,
All I know, and all unknown,
Given now to God alone.

Cho—Sweetly resting, doubting o'er,
All the Lord's forevermore,
Blood divine flows o'er my soul,
Sanctifies and makes me whole.

2 Take me Lord and all I have,
Take and to the utmost save,
All is on the altar laid,
All a perfect offering made.

3 Reckoning now this soul of mine,
On the strength of words divine,
Dead to sin—alive to God,
Thro' the spirit and the blood.

4 Not what I can do or be,
But what God can do in me,
Resting on his faithfulness,
Saved thro' Jesus' power and grace.

5 Faith has clasped the altar shrine,
Touched the nature all divine,—
Shout His praise through earth and skies,
Altar, Priest and sacrifice.

## 299

From "Gems of Gospel Song," with per.

Are you ready for the Bridegroom,
When he comes, when he comes?
Are you ready for the Bridegroom,
When he comes, when he comes?
Behold! he cometh! Behold! he cometh!
Be robed and ready, for the Bridegroom comes.

Chorus.
Behold the Bridegroom, for he comes, for he comes!
Behold the Bridegroom, for he comes, for he comes,
Behold! he cometh! behold! he cometh!
Be robed unready, for the Bridegroom comes.

2 Have your lamps trimmed and burning
When he comes, when he comes; &c.
He quickly cometh, he quickly cometh,
O soul! be ready when the Bridegroom comes.

3 We will all go out to meet him
When he comes, when he come; &c.
He surely cometh! he surely cometh!
We'll go to meet him when the Br'degroom comes.

4 We will chant alleluias
When he comes, when he comes, &c.,
Lo! now he cometh! Lo! now he cometh!
Sing alleluia! for the Bridegroom comes.

## 300

I'm a pilgrim and I'm a stranger,
I can tarry, I can tarry but a night,
Do not detain me, for I am going,
To where the streamlets are ever flowing.

Cho—I'm a pilgrim, &c.

2 Of that city, to which I journey,
My Redeemer, my Redeemer is the light,
There is no sorrow, nor any sighing,
Nor any tears, nor any dying.

# HIGHWAY HYMNAL. 125

## INDEX TO FIRST LINES BY NO.

| | No. |
|---|---|
| A better day is coming | 146 |
| A charge to keep I have | 83 |
| Alas and did my Saviour | 189 |
| All for Jesus | 89 |
| All hail the power of Jesus' name | 77 |
| All hands aboard | 120 |
| All my life long | 241 |
| All the world is on the breakers | 14 |
| All the promises of Jesus | 162 |
| Altar calls | 200 |
| Am I a soldier of the cross | 37 |
| And can I yet delay | 106 |
| And can it be | 203 |
| And now I have flung myself recklessly | 22 |
| An old soldier I stand | 9 |
| Are you ready for the Bridegroom | 299 |
| Are you standing on the Rock | 112 |
| Arise my soul arise | 81 |
| As I wandered sweetly musing | 5 |
| As Jacob once traveled | 164 |
| A soft sweet voice | 2 |
| At the sounding of the trumpet | 122 |
| Awake my soul | 202 |
| Awake, O heavenly wind | 227 |
| Awaken ye people and hear | 282 |
| Behold the Ark of God | 79 |
| Beneath the glorious throne | 95 |
| Blessed assurance | 25 |
| Blessed are the pure in heart | 194 |
| Blessed Jesus Thou art mine | 137 |
| Blest be the tie that binds | 152 |
| Bright scenes of glory | 49 |
| Broad is the road | 218 |
| But drops of grief can | 119 |
| But there is a spot | 280 |
| Came a voice to my ear | 6 |
| Children of the Heavenly King | 99 |
| Christ in me the hope for all | 209 |
| Christ was born in Bethlehem | 6 |
| Come believer, hungering, thirsting | 260 |
| Come every soul | 279 |
| Come on my partners in distress | 215 |
| Come sit down here beside me | 64 |
| Come thou Fount of every blessing | 5 |
| Come to Jesus | 276 |
| Come ye sinners, poor and needy | 28 |
| Come ye that love the Lord | 51 |
| Dear Jesus I long | 144 |
| Down at the Cross | 17 |
| Draw me nearer | 117 |
| Every boon that heaven can grant | 205 |
| Fade, fade each earthly joy | 91 |
| Faith hymns | 291 |
| Floods of mercy break around me | 242 |
| Forever here my rest shall be | 142 |
| From every stormy wind | 111 |
| Fly to the arms of the Saviour | 283 |
| God's car of salvation | 210 |
| Goliath the Philistine | 128 |
| Guide me O thou | 97 |
| Have you been to Jesus | 75 |
| Have you heard, have you | 213 |
| Hear my prayer | 230 |
| Hear the foot steps of Jesus | 238 |
| Hear the gentle voice that | 105 |
| He has washed away my sin | 90 |
| He leadeth me | 264 |
| Holy Spirit faithful Guide | 266 |
| How bright the hope | 70 |
| How dark and dreary | 8 |
| How firm a foundation | 289 172 |

| | No. |
|---|---|
| How happy every child of grace | 206 |
| How happy and joyful the hours | 214 |
| How happy is the man | 268 |
| How lost was my condition | 220 |
| I am coming to the Cross | 92 |
| I am dwelling on the mountain | 167 |
| I am fading away | 156 |
| I am saved the Lord hath | 45 |
| I am saved: Jesus bids | 86 |
| I am so glad that our Father | 251 |
| I am the vine | 193 |
| I am the vine said Jesus | 65 |
| I am waiting for Jesus | 191 |
| I am weary Lord | 7 |
| I am with thee every hour | 228 |
| I bring you tidings | 200 |
| I came to the spot | 121 |
| I dreamed last night | 118 |
| If there's any self in me | 72 |
| If you get there before | 27 |
| I gave my life for thee | 252 |
| I have a never failing bank | 224 |
| I have a Father in the promised Land | 141 |
| I have entered the valley | 176 |
| I have found repose | 153 |
| I have found the richest | 199 |
| I have long been a traveler | 198 |
| I have stood on the banks | 110 |
| I hear the Saviour say | 262 |
| I hear thy welcome voice | 93 |
| I know I love the better Lord | 243 |
| I know I'm trusting Jesus | 208 |
| I know I am born of the spirit | 148 |
| I know that my Redeemer lives | 295 |
| I love the Lord | 188 |
| I love to tell the story | 265 |
| I love thy kingdom Lord | 52 |
| I'm a pilgrim and I'm a stranger | 300 |
| I'm a pilgrim and stranger | 197 |
| I'm saved, Oh blessed Lord | 47 |
| I'm seeking a home | 73 |
| I'm saved I'm free | 133 |
| In God I have found a | 249 |
| In some way or other | 82 |
| In the Cross of Christ | 272 |
| In thy petty care of life | 131 |
| In the Rifted Rock | 190 |
| In the temple old | 44 |
| In the secret place | 71 |
| In the valley of sadness | 3 |
| I saw a blood-washed | 115 |
| I saw a happy pilgrim | 114 |
| Is there any sad heart | 245 |
| I storm the gate of strife | 223 |
| I thirst thou wounded | 139 |
| I've found a friend in Jesus | 178 |
| I've joined the army | 135 |
| I've launched my bark | 30 |
| I've reached the land of corn | 134 |
| I walk with Jesus | 16 |
| I will follow Thee | 180 |
| I will sing you a song of the Lord's | 166 |
| I will sing you a song of that beautiful | 261 |
| Jesus I my cross have taken | 284 |
| Jesus! Jesus blessed Jesus | 165 |
| Jesus! Jesus precious Jesus | 35 |
| Jesus, Lord I come | 15 |
| Jesus lover of my soul, Hide me | 177 |
| Jesus lover of my soul, Let me | 171 |
| Jesus my all to heaven | 267 |
| Jesus my Lord to thee | 26 |
| Jesus my Saviour to Bethlehem | 183 |
| Jesus thine all victorious love | 34 |
| Jesus thou hast bid me live | 298 |

| | No. | | No. |
|---|---|---|---|
| Joys are flowing | 24 | Sowing in the morning | 182 |
| Just as I am | 207 | Sweet bards may chant | 216 |
| Keep close to Jesus | 40 | Sweet hour of prayer | 271 |
| | | Swing low, sweet Chariot | 29 |
| Let us come to the light | 38 | Table hymns | 202 |
| Let us sing of his love | 76 | Take the name of Jesus with you | 212 |
| Like the lilies toiling not | 36 | Take the world but give me Jesus | 168 |
| Lord dismiss us | 98 | Thanks be to Jesus | 239 |
| Lord I am thine | 182 | The blood of Christ | 101 |
| Lord I care not for riches | 247 | The blood that flowed | 235 |
| Lord in the strength of grace | 127 | The Cross, the Cross | 60 |
| Loving Saviour hear | 273 | The day is past and gone | 269 |
| Mercy's gate stands open | 113 | The foxes have their dwelling | 43 |
| Mine eyes have seen | 174 | The great Physician | 286 |
| Must Jesus bear the cross alone | 13 | The gospel train is coming | 129 |
| My all to Christ is given | 138 | The holy war is raging | 230 |
| My Bible leads to glory | 149 | The judgment day is coming | 201 |
| My days are gliding | 275 | The King's highway of holiness | 100 |
| My Father is rich in houses | 234 | The Lord has pardoned all my sins | 107 |
| My Father's son Jesus | 294 | The Lord is the fountain of goodness | 68 |
| My God I have found | 189 | The old Israelites knew | 211 |
| My grace is sufficient | 102 | The Saviour is calling | 231 |
| My home in heaven | 12 | The Shepherd is tenderly calling | 80 |
| My heavenly home | 274 | The voice of the Lord | 195 |
| My hope is built | 254 | The world is over come | 85 |
| My latest sun is sinking | 256 | There is a fountain filled | 21 |
| My life flows on in | 151 | There is a fountain deep | 100 |
| My pilgrim days | 137 | There is a happy land | 249 |
| My soul be on thy guard | 84 | There is a spot to me more dear | 255 |
| | | There is an hour of peaceful rest | 270 |
| Near the Cross where | 74 | There is a realm that's | 50 |
| Now I feel the sacred fire | 19 | There'll be a rift in the azure dome | 41 |
| Now I lay me down | 248 | There'll be rest by and by | 48 |
| | | There's a fountain flowing | 287 |
| O, blessed fellowship divine | 143 | There's a highway for the | 173 |
| O, do not be discouraged | 250 | There's a land that is fairer | 232 |
| O, do not suffer | 285 | There's a question that comes | 87 |
| O, for a faith that will not | 225 | There's not a bright and | 170 |
| O, for a heart to praise my God | 222 | There was naught in God's world | 11 |
| O for a thousand tongues | 147 | This is the way I long | 108 |
| Of him who did salvation | 109 | 'Tis better to shout | 233 |
| O, glory land! O jubilee | 31 | 'Tis known on earth | 158 |
| O, glorious theme | 94 | 'Tis so sweet to trust in Jesus | 53 |
| O, God my heart doth cry to Thee | 57 | 'Tis the last call | 221 |
| O, God my heart doth long for Thee | 88 | 'Tis religion that can give | 253 |
| O, happy day | 125 | Thirsty soul thy Lord | 54 |
| O, how happy are they | 104 | Thou my everlasting portion | 187 |
| O, I have religion | 161 | Time speeds away | 219 |
| O, I left it all with Jesus | 204 | To-day if ye will hear his voice | 277 |
| O, mourner in Zion | 20 | To thee now dear Christ | 257 |
| O, my God how thy salvation | 58 | 'Twas Jesus my Saviour | 258 |
| O, now I see the crimson | 61 | | |
| One more days work for Jesus | 296 | Urge on your rapid | 281 |
| One sweetly solemn thought | 130 | Wake sinner wake! | 244 |
| On the carnal field of mammon | 196 | We may spread our couch | 159 |
| On the mountain top of vision | 175 | We're bound for the land | 186 |
| O, sometimes the shadows | 184 | What a friend we have in Jesus | 116 |
| O, sinner come without delay | 217 | What can wash away my sins | 64 |
| O, sinner come along with me | 62 | What poor despised company | 185 |
| O, tell the story | 32 | What subdued and conquered me | 67 |
| O, thou God of my salvation | 96 | What that voice | 163 |
| O, thou that sleepest, rise | 10 | When earth and flesh | 39 |
| O, the wonders of creation | 133 | When I can read my title clear | 220 |
| O, turn ye O, turn | 150 | When the clouds are gathering | 246 |
| Our flag has the hue | 1 | When the voyage of life | 46 |
| Our Father, who art in heaven | 42 | Where'er we meet you always | 140 |
| Our gracious Saviour and our Lord | 293 | While I'm kneeling by your side | 63 |
| O, what will it profit | 2 | While we bow in thy name | 103 |
| O who'll stand up for Jesus | 157 | Who, who are there besides | 154 |
| | | Why walk ye my brother | 4 |
| Praise God from whom | 23 | Why do these doubts and fears | 136 |
| Precious salvation so full | 237 | Will you come, will you come | 278 |
| Precious Saviour thou hast | 155 | Will you go, brother, go | 55 |
| | | Will your anchor hold | 297 |
| Redeemed how I love | 124 | With earth's adoring throng | 78 |
| Rock of Ages cleft for me | 280 | | |
| Sad and weary | 128 | Ye angels, who mortals attend | 228 |
| Sheltered in the Rock | 236 | Ye valiant soldiers of the Cross | 182 |
| Should the death angel | 181 | Ye who know your sins forgiven | 179 |
| Sow beside all waters | 56 | You may sing of the beauty | 263 |

www.ingramcontent.com/pod-product-compliance
Lightning Source LLC
Chambersburg PA
CBHW022137160426
43197CB00009B/1331